Extensio Dei –
Mission as Divine Reaching Out

Extensio Dei –
Mission as Divine Reaching Out

Jacob Kavunkal SVD

2020

Extensio Dei - Mission as Divine Reaching Out - Published by the Indian Society for Promoting Christian Knowledge (ISPCK), Post Box 1585, Kashmere Gate, Delhi-110006.

ISBN: 978-81-946569-4-4

Laser typeset by

ISPCK, Post Box 1585, 1654, Madarsa Road, Kashmere Gate, Delhi-110006 • *Tel:* 23866323

e-mail: ashish@ispck.org.in • ella@ispck.org.in
website: www.ispck.org.in

Contents

Preface

The title of this book could sound strange at least to some. Unpacking the word '*extensio*' one realizes that it is derived from the Latin verb *extendere* (to reach out) with its past participle, *extensus,* the root of the abstract noun *extensio,* to mean, reaching out or reaching toward. It is almost identical with another Latin term, *protendere,* reaching toward. Due to the familiarity in English of the word 'extension' I prefer to speak of *Extensio Dei,* Divine Reaching Out.

Arguably, one can wonder how *Extensio Dei,* differs from a similar term *Missio Dei,* that is in vogue since the Willingen Conference (1952). Willingen spoke of *Missio Dei* to show that God is the origin of mission and not the church. However, *Extensio Dei* goes beyond, in so far as God's very nature, as love, is reaching out. Hence, mission is the very identity of God and the church, as the continuation of that divine reaching out through Jesus Christ, also is Mission by its very nature, as shown by the Second Vatican Council that described God as "Fountain-like Love."

Even a casual reading of the Bible reveals how it is a narrative of the divine reaching out to humans and creation, beginning with the creation story. In an earlier book, *Anthropophany,* (manifestation of the human being) I focused on the human side of the divine reaching out, whereas here I try to show that the ground of the revelation of the human person is the self-effusive divine love.

My source is primarily the Bible, though I am influenced by other writers as well.

Portions of some of the chapters that follow have appeared earlier, elsewhere. I have reworked and modified them to be integrated here. The chapter on development contains a paper originally presented at a seminar at the Deakin University, Melbourne, and was included in the volume edited by Mathew Clarke and published by Continuum, London. Similarly, the chapter on Reformation and Vatican II was originally a paper read at a seminar on Jesus of Nazareth, organized by the Sydney School of Divinity, Sydney. I am indebted also to *Sedos Bulletin*, Rome and *Pacifica*, the journal of the University of Divinity, Melbourne, for including material originally published in those journals.

I am indebted to Siobhan Foster, BA, BTh, Dip.Lib., for her final editing of the chapters and thus making the book more reader friendly. My gratitude to ISPCK, Delhi and its General Secretay Revd Dr Ashish Amos, for publishing the book.

If the book enables the Christian community to appreciate its missionary vocation even in a small degree, the book will have accomplished its purpose.

Jacob Kavunkal, SVD

Abbreviations

AA.   *Apostolicam Actuositatem*, Vatican II's Decree on the Apostolate of the Laity.

AG.   *Ad Gentes*, Vatican II's Decree on Mission.

AL.   *Amoris Laetitia*, Pope Francis' Apostolic Exhortation on Love in the Family.

CA.   *Centesimus Annus*, Pope John Paul II's Encyclical Letter on Social Justice.

DV.   *Dei Verbum*, Vatican II's Dogmatic Constitution on Divine Revelation.

EG.   *Evangelii Gaudium*, Pope Francis' Apostolic Exhortation on the Proclamation of the Gospel.

EN.   *Evangelii Nuntiandi*, Pope Paul VI's Apostolic Exhortation on Evangelization.

FABC.   Federation of Asian Bishops' Conferences.

FC.   *Familiaris Consortio*, Pope John Paul II's Apostolic Exhortation on the Role of Christian Family.

GS.   *Gaudium et Spes*, Vatican II's Pastoral Constitution on the Church.

LE.   *Laborem Exercens*, Pope John Paul II's Encyclical Letter on Human Work.

LG.   *Lumen Gentium*, Vatican II's Dogmatic Constitution on the Church.

LS.   *Laudato Si'*, Pope Francis' Encyclical Letter on the Care for our Common Home.

MM.   *Mater et Magistra*, Pope John XXIII's Encyclical Letter on the Social Teachings of the Church.

NA.   *Nostra Aetate,* Vatican II's Declaration on the Relationship of the Church to other Religions.

OA.   *Octogesimo Adveniens,* Pope Paul VI's Encyclical Letter on Church's Social Teachings.

PP.   *Populorum Progressio,* Pope Paul VI's Encyclical Letter on the Development of Peoples.

PT.   *Pacem in Terris,* Pope John XXIII's Encyclical Letter on Peace on Earth.

QA.   *Quadragesimo Anno,* Pope Pius XI's Encyclical letter on Social Justice.

RM.   *Redemptoris Missio,* Pope John Paul II's Encyclical Letter on Mission.

RN.   *Rerum Novarum,* Pope Leo XIII's Encyclical Letter on Social Justice.

SC.   *Sacrosantum Concilium,* Vatican II's Constitution on the Sacred Liturgy.

SRS.   *Sollicitudo Rei Socialis,* Pope John Paul II's Encyclical Letter on Social Concerns.

UR.   *Unitatis Redintegratio,* Vatican II's Decree on Ecumenism.

Introduction

T he church has always been faithful to its call to continue the mission of Jesus Christ through its witness to him after his resurrection, even if the understanding and expression of that mission underwent changes in the course of history.

The very word 'mission' as we use it today, gained currency only with the colonial times. Until the end of the fifteenth century mission referred mostly to the inner relationship of God as Trinity, as explained by St. Augustine.[1]

When St. Ignatius of Loyola founded the Jesuit Order, to the normal three vows that the religious profess, he added a fourth one, "the Vow of Mission," to say that the members of the Order are prepared to discharge any assignment (mission) that the Pope would give. Since the founding of the Order almost coincided with the beginning of colonial forays, soon the word mission was understood as any exotic far-away places, adding the geographical connotation to mission. An associated idea was the 'frontier mission' where the actual engagement of fighting non-Christians to make them Christians, took place.

Vatican II, with its global perspective of renewal and *ressourcement*, spelt out the understanding of God as "fountain-like love" (AG 2), corresponding to the biblical narrative, and presented mission as an unfolding of this love (AG 2-9; LG 1-5). In this Vatican II proved to be a radical leap forward, as far as the concept of mission was concerned, even if not always the description of it. It is no more just a quality or a note of the church, as it was understood, but the church is mission, as the continuation of God as love, as mission.[2] God as mission, reaches out in creation, covenants, the different sendings and, ultimately, in God's word incarnate, Jesus Christ. The very identity of the church is its reaching out, mission defines the church.

In Jesus of Nazareth God manifests God's nature. Hence, evangelist John culminates the prologue to the gospel with the statement, "No one has ever seen God; the only Son, who is in the bosom of the Father, he has made him known" (1:18). This he accomplishes, according to the four gospels, by ushering in God's reign, and, thus, becoming God's presence, *shekinah*, in his boundary-breaking acceptance of all, more so of sinners, tax collectors, the excluded ones and having table-fellowship with them, in healing the sick, feeding the hungry, forgiving sinners, and above all by declaring the practice of love and compassion as the way to God rather than empty rituals and external ritual purity. This, in turn, angered the religious authority who with the help of the Roman rulers, killed him by crucifixion. But God affirmed him by raising him from the dead and making him the Messiah (Act 2:36).

Jesus of Nazareth's ministry was a practice of love as social transformation, not a political violence as the popular expectation was, though he himself was subjected to political violence and was killed. The God who raised Israel out of Egyptian bondage, and made it a "kingdom of priests, and a holy nation" for God (Ex 19:6), meaning that it has to become an agent of God's love that it had experienced, raised Jesus from the dead to be present in the church (Mt 28:20) to continue him as mission.

The church is mission in the framework of God's relationship to the universe, to humanity and history as manifested in the Bible, in Jesus Christ. The externalization and continuation of God as mission, cannot be introverted, finding its end in itself, but in extroverted service to the world, though as God's instrument of self-reaching out, there has to be an ecclesial community in every culture (Mt 20:19) to serve as the salt, light and leaven (Mt 5:13-16). Its vision has to be as wide as God's vision.

Moses received his call with the experience of God who had seen the affliction of the people and heard its cry (Ex 3:7), the God who informed him that God-self was ever-present love (Ex 3:14) and who wanted Moses to liberate the people from their bondage in Egypt. In the same vein Jesus of Nazareth experienced God at the time of his baptism with the anointing of God's Spirit, along with the words: "You are my well-beloved Son" (Mk 1:11. Cf also Mt 3:16-17; Lk 3:22; Jn 1:32-33), to proclaim God's Reign (Mk 1:15; Mt 4:17; Lk 4:1-19).[3] After the Resurrection this is continued through the church (Jn 20:17; 19-23).

The church can be faithful to its call to be missionary, only to the extent of its experience of the Lord and through him, God his Father and the Father's love. This can liberate it from the traditional one-sided perception of mission based on a moral psychology that says humans are all failed creatures needing the atoning death of Jesus. As explained by Peter in his very first address, Jesus was killed by the religious leaders as a result of his ministry, but was raised by God, making him Christ (Act 2:22-24, 36).

Jesus portrayed this love and this relationship of the Kingdom in terms of a wedding feast. The kingdom of God is not about power and domination, but gifting and honouring humans with the hospitality of God. This becomes tangible in the mission of the church.

Every human culture is permeated by divine providence (Amos 9:7). What the proclamation of the gospel brings about is the actualization, making present, of God's love in human terms as it happened in the ministry, death and resurrection of Jesus Christ. This way the church becomes a transforming agent in every culture. Every culture is affected by human selfishness making life miserable for fellow humans and equally for oneself as well. This has to be healed by the church's practice and proclamation of the divine love and compassion.

The gospel is not a culture, though gospel can be proclaimed and lived only through and in a culture, as was realized in Jesus of Nazareth, through the Jewish culture. However, already the apostolic church made it clear how the gospel is not to be identified with a culture, by stating that "no unnecessary burden is to be imposed on any people" (Acts 15:28), thereby declaring that the Gentiles do not have to conform to the Jewish culture.

Though the expressions of most of the doctrines and dogmas are cultural, the gospel is a story, the narrative of God reaching out to humans through God's Word, to be "God with us" (Mt 1:23) and who "went about doing good," (Act 10:38), healing all that were oppressed by evil. This has to happen in every culture. To quote the saintly Pope Paul VI: "For the Church, evangelizing means bringing the Good News into all strata of humanity, and through its influence transforming humanity from within and making it new" (*Evangelii Nuntiandi* 18).

Culture is the way of life of a people, to which it is bound, giving that people its identity. In this sense every culture has an autonomy, bestowing on every person the right to live his/her culture. The human nature created by God can unfold itself only in and through a culture. Yet, in so far as culture is human made it also has dehumanizing aspects, death-dealing elements. Here is the role of the gospel, to transform it, make it humanizing, as the expression of the divine reign.

One of the insights of contemporary thought on human nature is the radical insufficiency of isolated existence. It is in dialogue and relationship with others that humans reach their full potency. This has implications even for religious existence. Dialogue and interaction with the followers of other religious traditions enriches the Christian community in its life in a world where religious plurality is not confined to any particular region.

No religion, as a human reality, can fully manifest the ineffable divine Mystery. This is true of Christianity as well in so far as Christianity also has human limitations. No one particular human articulation of the divine Mystery or the human experience of that Mystery can be equated with the Mystery itself for the Mystery is infinite, while humans are limited. The reception and expression of the divine reality by humans will always be limited.

Similarly, one particular theology cannot exhaust the Infinite. This can prompt Christians to interact with the followers of other religions. Even when there is the divine self-revelation in Christ, the grasp and living of it can be enriched by the religious experience of others. In this, Christians are only in the biblical tradition in so far as the Israelites learned several aspects of their faith, such as the resurrection of the dead, the idea of creation, the faith in Monotheism, rather than the earlier Monolatry;[4] and others, during the Babylonian exile in interaction with the followers of the Babylonian religions, especially Zoroastrianism.

All these are only secondary reasons for the Christian to enter into dialogue with the followers of other religions. Above all, it is inherent in the Christian mission as reaching out to others as the expression of the divine self-reaching out. It is prompted also by the Kingdom-ministry of Jesus, in as much as in a world of religious plurality, peace and justice cannot be realized without the collaboration of all. This is implied also in the holarchical relationship, where each is a whole, while at the same time, part of a higher reality.

Despite the value of philosophical knowledge and reasoning, humans by themselves would never be able to know God without God making Godself known, including through creation which, according to Vatican II, is revelation in deed (SC 2). If so, any knowledge of God anywhere is integral to the divine self-manifestation and cannot be dismissed as the result of human pride, human beings trying to know and respond to God all by themselves. The many descriptions of the divine as well as the different ways of responding to the same, indicate primarily the infiniteness of the divine mystery. Consequently, the human response to that revelation has to be qualified as faith, in Christian terms. It is the beauty of the Jewish faith that it celebrated the faith of all peoples in terms of the universal covenant (Gen 9:8ff.).

It follows that the Christian faith has to outgrow even the Rahnerian position that, though it was a far-reaching understanding when it was suggested, the followers of non-Christian religions can be saved in and through their religions until they encounter Christ in an existential way. It has to be admitted that the Christian duty is not primarily to find out the possibility of salvation outside the church, but to follow Jesus. When the disciples asked Jesus if only a few would be saved (Lk 13:23), he was dismissive of the question as irrelevant and reminded them of their need to live the discipleship rather than claiming to have association with Jesus! On another occasion he tells the disciples how all those who do the will of God are his brothers, sisters and mother (Mk 3:35). Similarly, of the ten persons healed of leprosy, to the Samaritan, in contrast to the nine Jews, Jesus declared: "Go your way, your faith has made you well" (Lk 17:19).

The church's openness and respect for other religious traditions does not dispense it of its foundational call to witness to its experience of God in Jesus Christ as love ever reaching out, ultimately leading to the realization of the divine reign. Dialogue is listening and speaking, learning and sharing, being enriched and enriching. The church makes its own the words of its Lord, "Those who have seen me have seen God," (Jn 14: 9; 12:45). This is decisive to the historical existence of the church. It has no other business than trying to make God's presence experiential by "going about doing good" (Act 10:38), more so in relation to the poor and the marginalized of society. As Pope Francis underlines, the church has no excuse about not being close to the poor and to show creative concern and engage in effective efforts so that the poor can live with dignity (EG 207). "Our faith in Christ, who became poor, and was always close to the poor and the outcast, is the basis of our concern for the integral development of society's most neglected members" (EG 186).

Jesus navigates the two young men who approached him asking as to where he lived, into his world, with the words, "Come and see" (Jn 1:39). In Jesus they experienced the good shepherd who leaves the ninety-nine sheep and goes after the lost one, like a woman who sweeps the entire house to retrace a lost coin (Lk.15:3-10); like the landowner who wishes all to have the means of livelihood so as to hire workers even at the eleventh hour (Mt 20:1-16). The kingdom that Jesus proclaimed is a blessing for the poor, the mournful, the hungry, the voiceless as they experience the blessings of the kingdom through the struggle of the righteous by their compassion, their detached actions, and by their suffering for justice (Mt 5:3-11). Justice is the right of the defenceless!

The prayer that Jesus taught his disciples is an eminently missionary prayer (Lk 11:2-4; Mt 6:9-13). It expresses the kingdom vision, calling for holiness mirroring the divine holiness (Lev 19:2) to serve as light (Is 42:6; Mt 5:14), to do God's will,[5] asking food for the hungry,[6] seeking righteousness and forgiveness in the spirit of the Jubilee (Lev 25), and deliverance from all temptation and the evil-one that one comes across in daily life. In short, through this prayer a Christian prays for the realization of the divine household, the only purpose of mission. It can change the world of the one who prays it, even as the world of a merchant in search of a precious pearl is changed on finding the priceless pearl (Mt 13:45-46).

The church is an event of God's entry into human history as a human person, in Jesus of Nazareth. Jesus' proclamation of the Kingdom assumed expression in the local context, translating it in terms of the experience of the people, through the narratives of his words and deeds but always with the overarching theme of God's "fountain-like love." This contextual relevancy can be understood as the undying demand of his mission.

A tax burden imposed by agents of a foreign rule or the excommunication mandated by a religious authority to maintain ritual purity may not be the root cause of marginalization of many in the present age, as it happened at the time of Jesus. In contemporary society many become victims of marginalization and untold misery traceable to a host of reasons. Unrestrained craze to wield power, political, economic, social or even religious; the display of shields of caste, race, or national purity; the chase for pleasure and gratification of cravings of all sorts; dishonesty and intolerance and teaming up with religious fanatics letting loose a reign of terror and fear; ecological degradation, poverty, sickness or natural disasters; are only a few of the expressions of the burden and affliction of the poor in modern times.

Salvation, definitely, is a foundational theme in Christianity. In fact, it is the goal and striving of Christian faith. However, the salvation that Jesus proclaimed was not primarily other-worldly. Zacchaeus experienced salvation already when he responded to Jesus' teaching of sharing and love, forgiveness and acceptance (Lk 19:9). The law of the time commanded an adulterous woman should be stoned. Jesus' pronouncement, "Let him who is without sin be the first to throw a stone at her," with the accompanying assurance to the woman, "Neither do I condemn you; go, and do not sin again," manifests the expansiveness of the divine compassion affording the experience of salvation for the woman caught in adultery (Jn 8: 3-11).[7]

Salvation, in the Bible, is seldom about heaven, but it has more to do with earth. It is transformation of life already on earth. Exodus, the Jubilee, return from exile, are all expressions of salvation in the Bible. It is "the acceptable year of the Lord" that Isaiah predicted (Is 61:2) and that Jesus ushered in (Lk 4:18-19). It has to be emphasized how the prophet Isaiah comforts the Hebrews, returned from the Babylonian exile, that the Lord has forgiven their iniquity already (40:2), and comes with his might to rule the people (40:10).

One of the leading traumas of contemporary times is a sense of exile, exhaustion, estrangement or alienation from meaning in life, from God and from fellow humans. Both collectively and individually, humans stand in need of a return from this sense of alienation as the prodigal son returned and reinstated his relationship not only to the parent but to the elder brother, as well as to the land and society. Salvation is return and reconnecting,[8] which, in turn, ushers in light and serenity in one's life.

Obviously, salvation is also about food and drink, "You give them something to eat," instructs Jesus (Mk 6:37). Jesus not only multiplies bread for the hungry but also justifies the hungry disciples' plucking the wheat on the sabbath (Mk 2:23)!

The burden of sin is a mighty factor at all times. The message of the kingdom Jesus proclaimed begins with the invitation to repent (Mk 1:15) and he constantly assures the people he healed that their sins are forgiven as well (Mk 2:5,17; Lk 7:48). Forgiveness leads to a life of relationship with God and neighbours as shown in the story of Zacchaeus.

The kingdom of God is a transformation of life here on earth that will flow into hereafter. "Your will be done on earth as it is in heaven," is how the Lord taught the church to pray. The church has to make every effort that its presence becomes faithful to God's purpose for the world, to render its service meaningful and relevant.

When it is said that the biblical events are historical, it means not just that they really happened, but also it says what did they mean for the people of the time. As Marcus Borg suggests, given what their words meant for their *then*, what might their meaning be for our *now*?[9] For instance, what is the mission of the church today in the footsteps of Jesus feeding the five thousand, in contrast to Herod's serving the head of the prophet John in a dish (Mt 14:11 & 13-21)?

The chapters that follow pick up some of the above themes developing them as fitting expressions of mission for contemporary times, without any claim to be exhaustive, though. However, one point that permeates all the succeeding pages is mission. "You are the light of the world" (Mt 5:14), it is the clarion call. Light cannot, but radiate itself. The Book of Acts shows how the mighty works and words of Jesus were continued through the church (Act 5:12). That made Luke write the second volume, the Acts of the Apostles. Ultimately, it is all about the experience of and commitment to the person of Jesus Christ and his father.

Endnotes

[1] St. Augustine, *De Natura Boni 27*.

[2] Love by its very nature is reaching out (*extensio/protensio*)

[3] Though John does not begin with the explicit proclamation of the Kingdom, it is implied in 1:49-51; 3:19-21 and others.

[4] In the Bible strict Monotheism is affirmed only in post-exilic texts like Dutero-Isaiah, (Is 45:18, 22; 46:9), in contrast to the earlier assertions like: "Yahweh the God of Israel" (Ex 5:1) who is "a jealous God" (Ex 20:5).

[5] Expressing the emotion of the psalmist in Psalm 82:1-7.

[6] Reminding the many shared meals of Jesus culminating in the last supper as well as the instances of the multiplication of bread to feed the hungry.

[7] Some commentators thought the reason why this story was suppressed from the Johannine gospel at an early stage, was the fear that this unbounded compassion would encourage permissiveness in the community! Cf. Jennifer Knust & Tommy Wasserman, *To Cast the First Stone: The Transmission of a Gospel Story* (Princeton & Oxford, Princeton University Press, 2019), 96ff.

[8] Marcus J Borg, *Convictions* (London: SPCK, 2014), 68.

[9] Marcus J Borg, *Speaking Christian* (London: SPCK, 2011), 27.

Chapter - 1

An Alternate Reading of Genesis Chapter 3 and Mission

This chapter shows how Genesis chapter three, in contrast to the traditional interpretation that it is the description of the human fall and the origin of sin, allows an alternate reading. It points out, further, the implications of this new understanding for the theology of mission today.

Almost coinciding with the birth of the Bronze Age (ca 3500 BC) one of the first civilizations of the world arose, the Sumerian civilization, in Mesopotamia. The people that developed it are believed to have come from Iran. However, it was established in the midst of a people who dwelt in Mesopotamia as well as other parts of the Near East, such as western Arabia, Syria and Palestine, the Semitic peoples.

Tera, the father of Abraham, the Patriarch of the Hebrew people, belonged to this Semitic race. When he migrated from the Chaldean city of Ur to Haran (Gen 11:31), and later his son Abraham, to Canaan, naturally their mental baggage contained not only elements of Sumerian/Mesopotamian culture but its religious ideas as well which, eventually, were transformed and refined to be incorporated as part of the myths of the Bible (Myths understood as in comparative religions), in the context of the Exodus experience and the Covenant.

The migration of peoples in more or less 1900 BC served as the remote background of the oral traditions that, almost a millennium later, were assumed into the written text of the Bible.

The heart of the Exodus experience, the central and identity-creating event in the history of the Hebrews, was the Goodness of the God who delivered them from the Egyptian bondage, under the leadership of Moses. "I have seen their affliction, I have heard their cry" (Ex 3: 7), was the clarion call of this God. As Cardinal Walter Kaspar has pointed out, God's self-description to Moses in Exodus 3: 14, is: "I am always for you and with you," (and not, "I am Being", in Latin: Ego sum qui sum,[1] but in Hebrew, *hasa* and not *haya*.[2] It was the beginning, not only of their religious and national identity, but also of the religious text, the Bible. What is brimming all through the Bible is this Goodness of their God. The whole Bible is a narrative of God's love, reaching out. The biblical salvation history begins with Exodus, not with the creation story that we have in the book of Genesis. Genesis puts us in relation to the ancestors/patriarchs of the Israelites.

Though, traditionally Moses has been considered as the author of the first five books of the Bible, the Pentateuch, since the last quarter of the nineteenth century, based on the studies by scholars like Julius Wellhausen, it is universally acknowledged as the result of different sources.

Thus, contrary to the earlier perception of the book of Genesis as the work of a single author, giving a continuous history of the universe and of human kind, based on internal evidence and style, scholars agree on four sources: J (Yahwist), E (Elohist), P (Priestly) and D (Deuteronomist) which, probably at the time of Ezra (458-390), was collected and codified into a single book by a priestly author.

The different parts of the book of Genesis have not only different sources of origin but also different emphases and subjects. The first chapter of the Book of Genesis was written during exile by the priestly tradition, under the impact of the Babylonian creation myths, but always emphasising the uniqueness of the God of the Hebrews who not only created everything in six days but rested on the seventh day. Yahweh, the God of the Hebrews, is different from others, in so far as God rests on the Sabbath, making it sacred as well, which, one could say, is inspired by the Sinai covenant mandate to keep the Sabbath holy (Exo 20:8-11).

An important aspect of the priestly account of the creation of human beings in Genesis 1 is stated soberly: God blessed them saying: "Be fertile and multiply; fill the earth and subdue it…" (1:28). Further, God gave them the right to eat every plant and tree all over the earth as well as all animals of the earth and birds of the air (vs 29 & 30). God was pleased with God's creation that God found very good.

In contrast, when we come to the Yahwist account of the creation of humans in the next chapter, though God made a suitable partner for man (Gen 2: 18 & 22), the divine plan as expressed in the priestly account, namely, "being fertile and multiplying and filling the earth" (1: 28), remains inoperative in so far as man and woman lacked self-perception and the awareness of their gender difference and sexual potency, notwithstanding the declaration of the divine intent of marriage, where "a man leaves his father and mother and clings to his wife, and the two of them become one body" (Gen 2:24). The divine design of being fertile and filling the earth, according to the Yahwist account, is realized only through the events narrated in chapter three, underlining human accountability, described as the ethics of responsibility by the renowned Rabbi, Jonathan Sacks.[3]

Though there is an aspect of disobedience in 3:3, disobedience does not exhaust the meaning and purpose of the chapter, rather it has to be seen in context. Here is the challenge for the reader to be open to the unfolding of the narrative with its various nuances.

A major element of the chapter is the tree of knowledge of good and evil. The phrase "to know good and evil," frequently meant sexual maturity in Hebrew. Taken together with the snake, which symbolized fertility, and the mention of their shame at being naked, it seems clear that through all these, the author was connecting the fundamental human self-awareness and sexuality and achieving the divine plan of filling the earth that was expressed by the priestly narrative in 1:28. However, this is converted into reality through human choice and human collaboration, even as God gives humans the role of naming the animals of the ground and birds of the air (2:19). This is emphasized by a further assertion: "The man gave names to all the cattle, all the birds of the air, and all the wild animals" (2:20). By eating the fruit of the tree of knowledge through their own conscious choice, humans become aware of their nakedness (Gen 3:7), i.e. they come to the awareness of their sex difference as well as the purpose of it, they are not just partners or companions anymore.

The narrative continues to flow smoothly with God accompanying humans, showing further, how God prepared Israel's ancestors, beginning with Abraham.

The Yahwist narrative in Genesis chapter 3 also explains questions about human life such as: why women have pain in childbirth, why people have to work for a living, why we wear clothes, why people are ashamed when naked, why there is death, why snakes crawl on the ground.

Without considering this comprehensive outlook, it was held how Genesis chapter 3 was the description of sin and human concupiscence. The very term 'sin' occurs for the first time in the Bible, only in the context of Cain killing his brother Abel (4:7). The creation account of chapter one, which is of later origin, as we have seen, has no reference to sin.

The whole of the third chapter of the book of Genesis is shrouded in the mystery of sexuality, that has played an important role in most religions, either glorifying it like the Sumerian religion, or shunning it as a cause of suffering, like early Buddhism. Though the Bible has a glorifying approach to sexuality (Gen 1: 28; 2: 24), it explains sexuality and sexual attraction, by stating that humans realized they were naked, along with painful procreation, through the beguiling work of the serpent. This is subtly reflected also in the New Testament in so far as Paul imposes periods of abstinence (1Cor 7: 5f) or Jesus' speaks of making oneself a eunuch for the sake of the Kingdom of heaven (Mt 19: 12).

Sexuality and progeny in the Bible are a source of blessing. Accordingly, to be without progeny, to be barren, is seen as a matter of dishonour and shame. Not only do we come across songs of love in some of the Biblical books, but also the Song of

Songs is one of the canonical books of the Bible. Marriage and wedding celebrations are occasions of joy. Jesus went so far as to compare the kingdom of God to an eternal wedding celebration (Mt 22:1ff)! In the same spirit, some Jewish Rabbis explained how the sacred night of the Sabbath was the most appropriate time for marital intercourse, reflecting divine intimacy!

Sexuality and love are part of creation and are, thus, gifts of God's goodness. Even as creation, in general, is good, orderly and under control, as coming from God, so too must sexuality be. Humans are responsible for the world and sexual behaviour as they are made co-creators with God. They are God's deputies. They must exercise this wisely and prudently, according to God's plan. Further, as Joseph Blenkinsopp has underlined, "The Eden story is nowhere referred to in any pre-exilic text, that is, at any time prior to the Neo-Babylonian period."[4]

The expulsion of Adam and Eve from the garden, according to Genesis chapter three, is not because of human sin, as much as due to God's fear that the humans will become immortal like God by eating the fruit of the tree of life (Gen 3:24)!

True, the Yahwist takes into account the universal perception of the sexual weakness of humans, prompting to sin, affecting even key biblical figures like David. Under the influence of the Zoroastrian principle of Ahriman, the source of evil as opposed to Ahuramazda, the principle of light and goodness, and the Enuma Elish myth of Enkidu losing the gift of living forever through the intervention of a snake, the Yahwist attributes the eating of the fruit to the influence of the serpent, the principle of evil. The emergence of evil is subsequent to creation by God.

In Genesis 1-11, the deluge is the decisive event after creation, and not the eating of the fruit in Genesis 3:1-7. The deluge is an act of un-creation, in contrast to the creative process described in Genesis chapters one and two.

This should not belittle the sexual realism of the Yahwist picturing the profound wonder of sexuality with its joy, overshadowed by the agony of deviation and sin. All these are presented in broad strokes. Ultimately, it is all part of the divine mystery and the awesome human responsibility, as unfolded in the course of the God of salvation.

Such a broader understanding of Genesis chapter three could compliment the one-sided and sin-dominated interpretation of it, and it can lead to a deeper appreciation of the centrality of the divine goodness. Even if chapters one and three are originally independent, in the biblical context, they are complementary. Together, they bring out the divine goodness and faithfulness, along with human frailty and the tendency to sin, yet without disposing of human accountability. That is the role of Genesis chapter three.

Part 2 Theology of Mission Today

The Ministry of Jesus with its Consequence

What has been said holds immense significance for the mission of the church today. It is well known how mission in the past, almost exclusively, was contoured and justified by the presumed fall of the first parents risking the salvation of all humans. The Christ event was read nearly always as remedial to that loss. Anselm of Canterbury, thought to be the Father of western theology by some, went so far as to say that Christ through his blood purchased the souls back for God, that had become the possession of the devil when humans ate the apple at his bequest. Some scripture scholars, like Martin Kaehler, saw the gospels, especially that of Mark, as a passion narrative with an introduction, ignoring all the beautiful things Jesus did and said! Accordingly, it was said that the redeeming death of Jesus made up for the sin of the first parents and this made God reopen heaven for humanity[5]. The church became the depository and dispenser of that salvation. The church's mission was, primarily, to make that salvation available to all humans in every part of the world. Traces of that theology can be detected even in Vatican II's Mission Decree, *Ad Gentes,* when it states: "Though God, in ways known to God alone, … Church is the God intended means of salvation" (n 7), forgetting the very description of God as a "fountain like love" given a few paragraphs earlier (n 2).

Another shortcoming of the interpretation of the Christ-event by linking it to the fall of the humans in paradise, is that it is blind to the scientific data based on human fossils as well as human tools, that human beings existed almost for three million years whereas the whole of the biblical story, as we have seen, spans only for about 5000 years.

There is a radical need to return to the gospels and to the early church that hardly mentions original sin. The fresh approach to Genesis Three, outlined above, can place one on the same wavelength as that of Jesus. Since the time of the return from the Exile there was the hope of the One who would bring about the redemption and restoration of Israel, the Davidic Kingdom, even though the term messiah occurs only in Daniel 9:25. True, one could trace the earliest *promise* of the Messiah in the promise made to David by Nathan, the prophet (2 Sam 7:10-15), in the context of building a Temple for the Lord.

The Messiah is the promised one whom Yahweh would bring about and who would embody the identity and mission of Israel, to be a light to the nations. Through the prophet Isaiah the Lord spoke: "You are my witnesses, my servants whom I have chosen to know and believe in me and understand that it is I" (Is 43:10).

The kingdom-centred mission of Jesus can be understood only in the context of the Old Testament, beginning with the divine promise of establishing the kingdom forever (2 Sam 7:13). Since then there was the undying faith in God establishing God's reign, that will last forever, despite the setbacks suffered through selfish kings, the exile and foreign invasions, including that of the Greeks and the Romans.[6]

With Daniel, the Messianic expectations become more vibrant, with the hope for the One who comes like the God of Israel's scriptures, on the clouds (Dan 7:13). He will receive a kingdom that replaces the earthly kingdom of the beasts (Dan 1:2; 2:37; 7:6). God's eschatological kingdom in its eternal duration will actualize in the Messiah (Dan 2:44; 6:26).

Jesus concretizes the messianic expectations by announcing the arrival of the divine reign (Mk 1:14; Mt 4:17), linking it with the great biblical theme of the Jubilee Year, though now it is not just another Jubilee, but the Jubilee, "the acceptable year of the Lord" (Lk 4:19; cf. Lev 25:8ff). Jubilee was the good news primarily to the poor who had lost their land or who had become slaves. Jubilee retrieved the original equality that the Israelites had when they came to the promised land. Jesus spelt this out through his announcing the good news to the poor, proclaiming release to the captives, recovery of sight to the blind and setting at liberty those who were oppressed, through the power of God's Spirit (Lk 4:18-19). In the fourth gospel the Jubilee, the kingdom, is experienced through the deeds of light (Jn 3:16-21).

The biblical idea of salvation and the naming of God or Jesus as saviour has to be understood from this integral sense. No wonder, Cyrus the Persian king who sent Israelites back to their own land is called a saviour (Is 44:24 – 45:8). Similarly, Peter, in the Acts of the Apostles qualifies a man as saved because he is healed of being a cripple by the power of the risen Jesus (Acts 4:5ff).

Jesus makes God and God's reign actual, tangible. "Those who have seen me have seen God" says Jesus (Jn 12:45; 14:9) for he, as the one descended from God, is the only one who has seen God (Jn 1:18; 6:40, 46). By doing the Father's will and speaking the Father's word Jesus becomes the concrete presence of the Father.

Jesus Christ is the vibration of God, God's body language, one may say. Albert Einstein gave the relativity theory, i.e., reality, at the sub-atomic level, is a combination of matter and energy as shown by the perception of light as a shower of particles as well as a wave of energy. Historical Jesus is to be approached not only through the historical critical method, but also through certain 'waves' (*shem* in Hebrew), by looking into the overflow, breath, rhythm and the tenor of his entire ministry. The Father and the Father's reign was his *shem*, his vibration. This should modulate our mission today.

The idea of divine presence is a theme dear to the Bible. Already in Genesis chapter 3 we see how God was moving with humans (Gen 3:8). This divine presence becomes more articulate, especially at moments of human helplessness, such as during the Egyptian slavery (Ex 3:7) or during the Hebrew plight through the desert (Ex 40:38), and through many other ways, finally culminating in the Incarnation of God's Word in Jesus of Nazareth (Jn 1: 14), who is called "Emmanuel, God is with us" (Mt 1:23). The entire ministry of Jesus was not only an articulation of God's presence but simultaneously it was also a manifestation of the way humans become present to God and to each other (Lk 10: 37; Jn 13:34). Through this presence of love, the community of his disciples will produce the same fruit as did Jesus (Jn 15.1). In this connection we can appreciate Peter's summarizing of Jesus's ministry as going about doing good (Act 10:38).

Jesus did create a new community and entrust it with his own mission (Mk 3: 14-15), implying at the same time the need to have a community of the disciples in every culture to continue that mission (Mt 28: 19), nevertheless, Jesus never spoke of a loss of salvation for humanity or that his death was for winning the salvation back,[7] to be made available in the community, the church. Jesus explained the existence of evil not to a human fall, but to the work of an enemy who sowed the seeds of darnel among the wheat (Mt 13:24-30).[8] Jesus was ever led by the goodness of the Father, who makes his rain fall on the good and the evil alike (Mt 5:45), the Father who is concerned about the lost one, even as he is similar to an employer of labourers who does not want anyone to be unemployed so as to hire labourers even at the eleventh hour and paying all a just wage (Mt 20:1-16).

When asked as to what must be done to be saved Jesus quotes the love command from Deuteronomy (6:5) and Leviticus (19:18), (Lk 10: 25-28). Similarly, Jesus pronounces how salvation has come to Zacchaeus when the latter has followed the love command (Lk 19: 9), even before his death on the cross!

The logical consequence of his inclusive, compassionate, love-centred and forgiving ministry, in contrast to the practice of the then religious leadership, was the crucifixion. The litmus test of his passion is that he was put to death on a Roman cross, with the title "King of the Jews." The execution of Jesus cannot be separated from his ministry. That ministry attracted rejection by the religious leaders of the time, right from the beginning of his ministry (Mk 2:1ff). In a sense, Jesus prepared his own death by pouring out his energy and compassion on behalf of the poor and the outcaste, the sinners, the suffering, those on the margins. His commitment to justice, his proclamation of universal salvation (Lk 4:25-27), his prophetic mission, forgiving sins, all stirred up the powers of opposition that led him to the cross. He came to cast fire (Lk 12:49), the divine reign that challenges the listener to be open to all, and freeing us from a tribal view of a God who is exclusive, for the privileged, and sticking to rituals and purity.

The climax of Jesus' conflict with the religious authorities was Jesus' authority manifested in the solemn entry into Jerusalem fulfilling the prophecy of Zechariah 9.9, that the religious authorities understood (Lk 19:37-40). That was followed by the cleansing of the temple and teaching in the cleansed temple qualifying the then religious leadership as a den of thieves. "The chief priests, the scribes, and the leaders of the people, meanwhile were seeking to put him to death" (Lk 19:47).

Mission Today

The Christ event is a memory and a metaphor. It is the memory of the Incarnation and ministry of Jesus due to which he was executed at Jerusalem during Passover by the Romans at the behest of the religious authority but was raised by God and made Christ (Acts 2:22-32). It is at the same time a metaphor inviting the disciples to follow his path holding his identity, his message and his mission. At the heart of the gospels is the element of conflict leading to death, resurrection and mission.

The Christian reading of the Bible and approach to mission today, must be contoured by the divine passion for compassion, divine love that is communicated in creation and in the Incarnation. Hence, the Divine Mission began with creation and not with Incarnation. Even as creation was the divine reaching out (*extensio*, in Latin), through God's Word and Breath/Ruah, Christ event was God's self-revelation on human terms (Jn 1:8; 12:45; 14:9). It shines all through the ministry. Zacchaeus, seen as evil, wicked and sinner, becomes significant for God, for he too is a son of Abraham (Lk 19:9). The least meritorious become significant for God.

Biblical narratives, unlike a book on cooking, with its direct meaning, have a depth of inexhaustible meaning that has to be plumbed out. There is always room for further insight and understanding. One need not limit oneself to the past interpretation of Genesis chapter three as a narrative of fall, sin and punishment, but can see it from the perspective of "the fountain-like love of God" (AG 2). Bible is faith stories, stories of God's action in history, rooted in the culture of the people to whom it was revealed. They help one to encounter God, a God who has carved humans in his palms (Is 49:16) and who like a hen tries to bring all under its wings (Mt 23:37).

For the earliest Christians, mission was sharing of an experience. "That which was from the beginning, which we have heard, which we have seen with our eyes, which we have looked upon and touched with our hands, concerning the word of life, the life was made manifest, and we saw it, and testify to it, and proclaim to you the eternal life which was with the Father and was made manifest to us, that we have seen and heard we proclaim also to you…" (1 Jn 1:1-4). In the light of the resurrection of the Lord the followers of Jesus felt empowered and impelled to share their experience of discipleship.

Scripture scholar John Shelby Spong has argued: "What the gospels tell is the presence of God in a contemporary moment, they interpreted this moment by applying to it similar moments in their sacred story when they were convinced the presence of God had also been real to their forebears in faith … That was the only way they could understand and process the God presence they found in Jesus that was so powerful."[9]

Mission today has no other motive than what late Pope John Paul II has said, "To serve human beings by manifesting the love of God made present in Jesus Christ" (*Redemptoris Missio* 2). In this the Pope was only true to the concluding instruction of Vatican II's Pastoral Constitution *Gaudium et Spes*: The church "will share with others the mystery of the heavenly Father's love" (GS 93), and make all aware of the divine salvation and respond to it.

Obviously, the practical expressions of this service of love, respond to the context. In a religiously pluralistic context like most parts of Asia, the priority will be Inter Religious Dialogue. Where justice is trampled upon and human dignity is thrown to the winds, mission primarily will be an involvement for prophetic justice and advocacy for the margins. It could be empowerment in different forms, and caring for the sick, the lonely, and for creation. It calls for the creation of new communities where they are not existing. In all this, the Christian community tries to be "the letters of Jesus Christ" (2 Cor 3:2) or "the aroma of Christ" (2 Cor 2:15), thereby becoming "the light to the world"

(Mt 5:14). The Christian community becomes the Sacrament of the divine salvation, divine reign made present in Jesus Christ.

As the recent Magisterium of the Catholic church, especially Pope Francis, has taught, the church has to become the carrier of the Goodness of God, inviting all to respond to this Goodness, by being good to one another. "The heart of its message will always be the same: the God who revealed his immense love in the crucified and risen Christ" (EG 11).

Endnotes

[1] Kaspar Walter, *Mercy: The Essence of the Gospel and Key to Christian Life* (New York: Paulist Press, 2014), 129.

[2] Julian of Norwich had spoken of the identity of God's Being as God's love. Love is not something God has or a property of God. Cf. Brant Pelphrey, *Christ Our Mother: Julian of Norwich* (London: Darton, Longman & Todd, 1989), 25.

[3] Jonathan Sacks, *To Heal A Fractured World: The Ethics of Responsibility*, London: Continuum, 2005. One of the challenging ideas of the Bible, as Jonathan Sacks describes, is that God invites humans as partners in the work of creation: naming, tilling, caring for the earth, procreation and others revealing God's faith in humans.

[4] Joseph Blenkinsopp, *Pentateuch: An Introduction to the First Five Books of the Bible* (New York: Doubleday, 1992), 64-65.

[5] The protagonists of the fall and atonement theology do not realize that the very fact of procreation is the result of the eating of the fruit. Without that heaven would not be populated except for Adam and Eve!

[6] Cf. Tim F. LaHaye and Ed Hindson (eds), *Exploring Biblical Prophecy from Genesis to Revelation* (Eugene, Oregon: Harvest House Publishers, 2011).

[7] Though Jesus in the Markan gospel, as in other gospels as well, constantly seeks to make the Father and Father's reign known, and that he was the path to be followed by the disciples (Mk 10:35-45), the church had to wrestle with the problem why, innocent though he was, was put to death. This brings in the idea of the "ransom" (Mk 10:45) even as the servant's death in Isaiah 53:10 is an "offering for sin". In the same way Paul, struggling to reconcile Jesus's death on the cross with the Deuteronomist pronouncement of curse on the one hanging on the tree (Dt 21:23), would say "Christ ransomed us from the curse of the law by becoming a curse for

us" (Gal 3:13). This is similar to the dialogue in the Matthean story of Jesus' baptism by John. In Mark we have the primitive story of the baptism. But to overcome the embarrassing aspect of the Messiah going through John's baptism of repentance, Matthew introduces the dialogue between Jesus and John justifying Jesus' baptism only "to fulfil all righteousness" (Mt 3:14-16).

[8] Neither did the followers of other religions ever believe that they could be saved only through the church and not through their own religions.

[9] John Shelby Spong, *Liberating the Gospels: Reading the Bible with Jewish Eyes* (San Francisco: Harper Collins, 1996), 19-20.

Chapter - 2

Mission an Epiphany of Love and Service

Vatican II's mission decree *Ad Gentes*, having outlined the basic theology of mission, firmly building it on the very nature of God, and having defined what is mission work proper, concludes the section by stating: "Missionary activity is nothing else and nothing less than a manifestation or epiphany of God's will, and the fulfilment of that will in the world and in world history" (AG 9). This will is presented in the opening paragraph of the section as "that fountain of love or charity within God the Father" (AG 2). The next chapter that describes mission work as such begins by stating again: "Sent by Christ to reveal and to communicate the love of God to all people and nations ..." (AG10).

Accordingly, the Council's greatest contribution was not only the retrieval of the missionary nature of the church, but also the anchoring of the same in the love of God, through the very conciliar process of *ressourcement* from the Bible and the fathers of the church. In this chapter, I wish to develop this theme of divine love and to emphasize how the church's mission today basically is a manifestation of this love actualized in service and that must assume priority over all other motives.

The New Context

Before we go into the new nuances in mission today it is imperative that we begin with some observations regarding the situations that are different from the times of Vatican II. In this we are only following the spirit of the Council that was convened by its architect, John XXIII, to make the church ever suited to proclaim the Word to the contemporary world.

In contrast to the Europe/West centred[1] church of Vatican II with the priority of sending personnel and resources to the 'missions', today we experience the presence of Christianity along with the followers of other religious traditions, anywhere in the world, due to the globalization process and mass migration. The multi-religious situation, even with a spirit of renewal and self-assertion, has become a reality everywhere. On the one hand no specific region today can be described as non-Christian, as Vatican II understood it, and on the other the former mission-sending regions are depleted of their personnel and financial resources, not to mention of their very Christian faith.

The post-colonial revival of the religious traditions of the world along with the respect for religious pluralism may be interpreted as a sign of the time. This, along with the socio-economic and political now of the world, indicates the inadequacy of *Ad Gentes'* approach to mission as "proclaiming the gospel and planting the Church among peoples or groups who do not yet believe in Christ" ("certain territories") (AG 6). We need to retrieve the spirit of the Bible that can be appropriated as good news for all the peoples of the world and we need an ecumenism that does not exclude any people. True, the church cannot bury its identity as a call to serve as the light and salt to the world (Mt 5:13-15); rather, as we shall see soon, it is an invitation to return to the kingdom-centred ministry of Jesus.

Another significant change in the world scene, starting already from the last days of Vatican II, is the growing phenomenon of secularization, affecting the regions considered to be 'Christian', the most. The gradual loss of a sense of the Transcendence manifested in different symptoms such as the decline in church attendance and the abandoning of religious practices, along with the chase after pleasures, can be described as the most acute concern for the Christian community.

A further major aspect of the contemporary world that can be seen as a positive sign of the time is the 'rise of the little ones of the world' by which I mean the rising awareness of people at the periphery of human society, of their human dignity and human rights, along with the unrest fuelled by the determination to regain the same[2]. Considering the kingdom-driven mission of Jesus as we have in the gospels, probably this is the greatest challenge for the church's mission today.

Creation, God's Reaching out in Love

The whole Bible is a narration of the manifestation of divine love, beginning with creation (Gen 1-2). Creation, as Iosif L. Bosch has shown, is God's "coming out to the other- is an image of the erotic divine creative impulse."[3] Obviously it is an act of divine self-reaching out. Iosif Bosch continues: "The text refers to the act of creation itself, in which God by natural and ecstatic love (*eros*) gives place to the other."[4]

The image of the Spirit brooding over the waters (Gen 1:2) further brings out this idea of love. Feminist theologian Elizabeth Johnson, quoting St. Augustine, invites our attention to this brooding over saying it is the way birds brood over their eggs, "where that warmth of the mother's body in some way also supports the forming of the chicks through a kind of influence of her own kind of love."[5] "The notion of a warm maternal bird fostering and cherishing the growth of her young, actually engendering them into existence by the loving power of her own body, provides an apt animal metaphor for the creative work of the Spirit of God, Giver of life."[6] Quoting several texts from the Wisdom literature, Elizabeth Johnson goes on to say, "Biblical wisdom literature's language about Sophia celebrates the one God's gracious goodness in creating and sustaining the world and in electing and saving Israel, and does so by drawing on the female image of the divine."[7]

Wisdom's act is not a one-time event, insists Elizabeth Johnson, rather the "bounteous love more mobile than any motion, the mystery of the Creator Spirit, utterly transcendent, dwells at the heart of the evolving world in its living and dying, empowering its advance ... The poetic images of the Bible offer a way for thought and feeling to grasp the expansive presence of God in the world as infinite, life-giving love."[8]

In so far as the nature of love is reaching out, we can approach the same mystery of creation as well as the rest of the biblical narrative as a process of divine self-reaching out, as an unfolding of the divine being. It is God's going out of God's self, in love. It can be described as God's ecstasy, *ex stare* – stepping out of oneself. Diarmuid O'Murchu rightly describes creation as the divine dance, a spontaneous and graceful movement.[9] What is to be underlined is that God's reaching out to the world in creation is not a second moment or an attribute of the divine being but just an expression of God's very being, Love. As Catherine La

Cugna has argued, "God's To-Be is To-Be-in-Relationship."[10] The whole biblical discourse can be encapsulated in one phrase: *Extensio Dei* (*extendere*=to reach out), divine self-reaching out.

The Bible continues the story of the divine love in the process of the making of the covenants as well as the sending of the judges, prophets, and ultimately God's Word Incarnate, Jesus the Messiah. Likewise, the whole Exodus event, leading to the formation of Israel as a nation chosen for a special service (Is 42:6, 49:6), begins as God's response to the affliction of the Hebrew slaves in Egypt and to their cry (Ex 3: 7, 9).

Commenting on the revelation of God's name "I am" (Ex 3:14), Walter Kasper writes:

"I am with you in your distress and I will accompany you on your way. I hear your cries and I answer your pleas. Correspondingly, the revelation of God's name is immediately connected with the ratification of God's covenant with the patriarchs and with the classic formulation of the covenant: "I will take you as my people, and I will be your God" (Ex 6:7). In the revelation of his name, God thus enunciates his innermost reality: God's being is present for his people and with his people."[11]

Kasper further shows how God's name is associated with the Hebrew root *hasah* which means to love passionately, rather than *haya* (to be), as many authors regard it.[12] "God's being is Being-for-his-people; God's being as Pro-Existence is the wonderful mystery of his existence," explains Ulrich Wilckens.[13]

This love is the core of the basic *shema* of the Israelites that Jesus quoted (Mk 12: 29-31 and par) combining Dt 6:4 and Lev 19:18. The two key words of the *shema* are *ahavah* (love, affection) and *hesed* (long-acting love), both of which, thus, are associated with love.[14] The Lord through the prophet Isaiah assures Israel: "Though the mountains be shaken, and the hills be moved, yet my unfailing love - *hesed* - for you will not be shaken (Is 54.10).

This dynamism of divine love is expressed in the universe, in life on earth, so complexly with different patterns, with certain interdependence, shaping a mind-boggling spectrum that Charles Darwin described as the "grandeur" of life,[15] and all following laws laid down by the author of the universe. Biblically speaking, this elaborately constructed web of life, each part so different from others, is the manifestation of the divine reaching out, divine love that acts even in every step of the self-organizing systems like a cell that interacts with the environment. The divine self-transcendence bestows even on single-celled organisms an innate ability to transcend themselves, which I would describe as the root of evolution. Jesus' words, "not a sparrow is forgotten before God" and "even the hairs of your head are all numbered" (Lk 12: 7) can be read in relation to this reality.[16]

What is so vital for our times, tending to a loss of sense of the Transcendence, is the urgent need to become aware of the mystifying presence of the divine in and around us, inviting us to respond through a sort of prophetic contemplation that is not only awe inspired but also committed to the dignity of life in every form, but above all, to human life. Denis Edwards rightly points out that Physicist Stephen Hawking's well known question: What is it that breathes fire into the equations and makes a universe for them to describe,[17] cannot be answered without reference to this "immanent energy of love."[18]

The Mission of Jesus

The divine self-reaching out in history is continued in the Incarnation of God's word in Jesus of Nazareth, as pointed out in *Dei Verbum* 2[19]. John the Evangelist brings out the link between the Old Testament understanding of creation and the New Testament. The word, through whom everything is created and enlightened, becomes human. According to the Johannine Prologue the creative activity is the first phase of the word (1:1-5) and through incarnation, the second phase of the activity of the word, we come to know the nature of the divine (1:18, see also 12.46 & 14:8). Dean Fleming elaborating the mission of God from the Johannine perspective writes: "Jesus' whole mission is a concrete expression of the loving character of God. For John, Jesus' words and works, his witness and his acts of service, his dwelling among us and his dying for us, are all seamlessly woven together as manifestation of divine love."[20] Francis J. Moloney, developing the theme of love in the gospel of John has drawn our attention to how at the heart of John's account of Jesus' final evening with his disciples, narrated in five chapters, taking a quarter of the entire gospel, is love: as it is acted out (13: 1-38), as it is spoken of (15:12-17) and as it is prayed for (17: 1-26).[21] This, in turn, prepares for the final "glorification" of the Father by manifesting the extent of his love (3: 16-17) through Jesus' self-surrendering death on the cross and thus accomplishing his task (19:30).[22]

Elizabeth Johnson has invited our attention to the incarnate word who, through his parables such as that of the lost coin, the lost sheep, hiring the servants at different hours of the day, and many others, taught that "the compassionate love of God is extravagant, transgressing all cultural religious expectations of fairness in order to gather in, every lost, hurt or rebellious sufferer."[23]

The teachings of Jesus are centred on love. In his sermon on the mount Jesus reminds us how he has come to *fulfil the Law* (Mt 5:17) and later, asked by one of his listeners as to which was the greatest law Jesus replies: "you shall love the Lord with all your heart… This is the first. The second is like this: you shall love your neighbour as yourself" (Mt 22:37-40).

In Jesus, God acts, revealing to humans the depth of his love. Gerald O'Collins points out how Jesus exercised the divine compassion, behaving and speaking in a way that forces us to the conclusion: "Jesus identified himself with the divine concern to forgive and save sinful human beings. Just as he understood his word and God's word to be identical, so he understood his presence and God's salvation to be identical."[24] For O'Collins the ministry of Jesus was "aimed above all to provoke a response to the loving and demanding presence of God."[25] That ministry earned Jesus the nickname "a glutton and a drunkard," and "a friend of tax collectors" (Lk 7:35).

The Synoptic gospels in particular portray Jesus' consciousness of being sent to communicate and enact with unique authority the divine reign, the realization of God's love. The many miracles are signs of the powerful actualization of the compassionate love of God. Biblically speaking, God is to be understood through God's word in creation and in his ministry, that was a process of gathering and transformation, and this Jesus described as God's reign.

Even the death and resurrection are also to be situated in the context of the divine love, rather than the atonement angle. God's passionate love that does not tolerate the manipulation of religion by the religious leaders of the time, without allowing space and time for human beings was active in the ministry of Jesus and the religious leaders tried to eliminate him by crucifixion. However, God raised him and affirmed him to be the Christ (Acts 2:22-24). Walter Kasper described the suffering and death of Jesus on the cross as "the unsurpassable self-definition of God."[26] Denis Edwards commenting on the various words used in the New Testament to communicate what God does for humans in Jesus Christ, words like salvation, redemption, reconciliation, sanctification and similar ones, writes: "It seems that for the New Testament authors, this rich variety was necessary because no one image or concept was sufficient to express what is finally beyond all our words: God's love poured out for us in Jesus' life, death, and resurrection and the giving of the Spirit."[27] God's love is the coherent account of the meaning of Jesus' life, death and resurrection.[28]

Jesus' mission is to be understood primarily as the very expression of the nature of God. Therefore, at the end of his ministry, in the fourth gospel, he exclaims: "those who have seen me have seen the Father" (Jn 14:9; 12:45). His ministry has to be seen not only as that of the sent one, but more so as the mission of the Son, with the awareness of his loving intimacy with God. The Johannine farewell discourse embracing chapters 14 through 16 is an articulation of the relationship between Jesus and the Father as well as between Jesus and the disciples, a relationship of perfect love and unity like the vine and the branches (Jn 15:1-10).

Message of Love

Following the biblical thought the Council has initiated the process of the retrieval of the divine love as the fulcrum of Mission theory and practice for our times. In this the Council anticipated what Christopher Wright, the author of the massive volume, *The Mission of God: Unlocking the Bible's Grand Narrative,*[29] points out: "Biblical mission and biblical hermeneutics seemed to morph into each other in unexpected but fascinating ways". Wright shows further how "Mission is what the Bible is all about; we could as meaningfully talk of the missional basis of the Bible as the Biblical basis of mission."[30] That mission is the diffusion of the divine love.

Just before the establishment of the covenant with Israel (Ex 20-24), Israel is told how it is made God's treasured people, so that "you shall be to me a kingdom of priests and a holy nation" (Ex 19: 6). Ross Blackburn has argued how the revelation of the biblical law in Exodus 19-24 is an expression of the generosity of God, implying that the divine righteousness is to be reflected in the lives of the people, who shall be holy (Ex 22:27). This in fact underlines the very formation of a specific people.[31] The creation of the new community, the church, is the continuation of the same mission, with its call to be the salt, light and leaven to the world (Mt 5: 13-15). The First Letter of Peter, having told the Christian community how it is to lead a holy life based on love, almost verbatim repeats Ex 19: 9, "You are a chosen race, a royal priesthood, a holy nation, God's own people that you may declare the wonderful deeds of him who called you out of darkness into his marvellous light" (1Pt 2:9).

In the Bible the way God sees is, "not with the eyes but with the heart – the heart in the biblical physiology being the seat of understanding rather than of feeling."[32] The four gospels tell us how Jesus was a spelling out of this heart of God. Though we may never come to know about the physical appearance of Jesus, we cannot miss the window to God's heart in Jesus that made people exclaim, "we never saw anything like this" (Mk 2:12). This language of the divine heart is outlined in the Sermon on the Mount: the ability to mourn with the mourning, to be the voice of the voiceless, to be in solidarity with those who hunger and thirst for justice, to act disinterestedly (i.e. without selfish motives), to be compassionate, to make a peace with justice.

Any reflection on mission today in the spirit of the Bible and of the Council can be guided by Archbishop Dennis Hart's advice: "Evangelization is not imposing our ideas, our beliefs on others, but showing the joy of God's love."[33] Love is **presence** and evangelization requires the presence of the Christian community in every culture (Mt 28: 19-20). Pope Francis reminds us: "Help the Church to grow through a life of attraction: without the preoccupation of proselytization."[34] The existence of the community is precisely for "apostolic initiative," as Pope Paul VI reminded the church (EN 24).

This task of apostolic initiative, evangelization, begins with the Christian quality of the community that can be qualified as presence (*Shekinah*=divine presence). This is enshrined in the very self-perception of the church of its identity as "the Sacrament" of the kingdom, "of intimate union with God, and of the unity of all humankind" (LG 1) and becoming on earth, "the initial budding forth of that kingdom" (LG 5). This reflects the early church's awareness of itself as a call to serve the world as its animating force: "What the soul is to the body Christians are to the world."[35]

Through its exercise of love and service the church becomes a sort of "soft-power" for the transformation of modern culture to make it more other-centred even as it did in the early centuries when it exercised a formative influence on European culture and civilization. "Without this Christian impulse, neither the cultural and social history of Europe nor the history of humanity can be understood," argues Walter Kasper.[36] Kasper goes on say that the most serious criticism that can be levelled against the church today, is the accusation that oftentimes only a few deeds follow its words of love and service.[37] This in turn invites the church to come down from its high moral stands to feel with the people of our times. What Archbishop Diarmuid Martin said in the context of the overwhelming approval of the gay and lesbian marriages in the Irish referendum, that it was an invitation to the church for a "reality check,"[38] is true for the whole church.

As missiologist Mary Motte, belonging to the Franciscan Missionaries of Mary, reminds us, "The awareness of God's sustaining love and creative power leads us to a missionary spirituality that is basically contemplative. By this I mean a spirituality that regards everything from the view that God's love is a creating love, embracing all persons and all creation. This is God's plan for creation; namely, that all be saved (cf Tim 2:11)."[39] The basic catholic perspective is to visualize the world as charged with the grandeur of God, "Grace is everywhere."[40]

This contemplative spirituality though a gift, is a task as well. The Christian presence is a compassionate presence in the spirit of following Jesus who began his ministry by quoting Isaiah 61:1-2 (Lk 4:18-19). Jesus as the Incarnation of the divine reaching out, reached out to the poor of his times; and we in turn have to bring the good news of God's liberation, God's reign to the poor of our times by offering space for persons and groups that are different from society's "expectation." People believing and worshipping differently than us, people with different eating, sexual, cultural feeling and tendencies have to find acceptance from us even as Jesus accepted the woman caught in adultery.

Transcendence is the movement from self-centredness to God-centeredness, from self-perspective to divine perspective. The God of the Bible transcends all and that is the challenge for the Christian mission today. God's call to Abraham to leave the Chaldean capital Ur to become a blessing to the nations (Gen

12: 1-3) is continued in the call of the Christian community. The Jewish theologian Abraham Joshua Heschel is right in saying that biblical religion is, "the awareness of God's interest in humans, the awareness of a covenant, of a responsibility that lies on Him as well as on us. Our task is to concur with His interest, to carry out His vision of our task."[41]

What is unfolded in the ministry of Jesus is this divine transcendence, requiring that we make the divine project of love rather than a passion narrative the corner stone of our mission theology. Despite the human limitations the church has to endeavour to follow Jesus, the path, in his ministry. The church becomes the embodiment of the love and service shown by Jesus. This can be described as an incarnational mission. As Ross Langmead has argued, "incarnational mission is not only a powerful metaphor but an essential ingredient in any proper model of Christian mission."[42] Incarnational mission is a "Christopraxis" (Ross Langmead), a radical and whole-of-life response in discipleship, making the loving, saving God present to the world, through our radical following of the Lord, in his compassion, concern, forgiveness, healing, feeding, accepting, hospitality, teaching, praying: in short, "to be with him and to be sent out" (Mk 3:14).

Unlike the current popular phrase, *Missio Dei*, prevalent especially among the protestant circles, Vatican II traced the very existence of the church back to the missionary nature of God, making the church missionary by its very nature. While *Missio Dei* tries to emphasize that mission is God's and not of the church, Vatican II asserts how mission is the very being of the church. Vatican II goes beyond what some have said, that mission has the church, and asserts: church is mission even as God is mission.[43]

This has huge implications for mission today. Mission can no longer be confined to one or the other elements of mission like proclaiming the gospel, or planting the church or saving souls nor can it be limited to any particular place. Mission has but one purpose, as John Paul II wrote: "to serve human beings by manifesting to them the love of God made present in Jesus Christ" (*Redemptoris Missio*, 2). That is the *raison d'etre* of the church in so far as it is the continuation of the divine self reaching out. This makes every Christian a missionary, without denying the role of those who make mission their specific charisma.One of the major consequences of this return to the biblical sources of mission is that mission is not directed to any particular people (*Ad Gentes*=followers of other religious traditions) but to the entire human kind and the cosmos, for God is the "true Mother of life and of all things."[44] God's loving presence with human beings remains the primary focus of the election of a specific people like Israel or later the community of the disciples of the Lord, the church. Neither the Sinaitic covenant nor the New Covenant in Jesus Christ cancels the universal covenant. This makes mission much more than opening the taps of salvation for non-Christians, partners in God's universal covenant, but drawing all back to the love of God through the community's love and service, the community's following the path of Jesus Christ. Mission is not primarily rocketing people into heaven as much as the transformation of this world.

Epiphany of Service to the World

The spirit of renewal and ressourcement initiated by Vatican II can prompt us to make a shift in mission from the intellectualistic and dogmatic approach, typical of the Greek mind-set, to that of the biblical narrative, one of love and compassion. "God is love" (1 Jn 4:8,16). The church has to spell out this love in the contemporary context through its service. Pope Francis reminded the bishops that they are to be "men who are guardians of doctrine not in order to measure how far away the world lives from the truth it contains, but in order to attract the world, to enchant it by the beauty of love, to seduce it with the offer of the freedom which is given by the Gospel."[45]

Jesus was not a temple person but declared how God is to be worshipped not in the temple but in the world in spirit and truth (Jn 4:21). God is to be served in the arena of the world where people are. God is inviting us to serve God in the world by caring for men and women in the world, especially those who are suffering in any form. As Karl Rahner, writing in the context of the Sacraments, reminds us, "rather than entering a temple which walls off the holy from the godless world outside, man sets up in the open expanse of God's world a sign proclaiming that not in Jerusalem alone, but everywhere in spirit and truth, God is adored and experienced."[46]

Service to the world renders a certain secularity to mission. Pope Francis reminds us how the church, as the house of the Father, has to reach out to everyone without exception, "but above all the poor and the sick, those who are usually despised and overlooked" (EG 48), for "the poor are the privileged recipients of the Gospel."[47] This demands a readiness to be "bruised, hurting and dirty," to be "out on the streets" rather than remaining "at the centre" (EG 49). In his encyclical *Laudato Si* the Pope argues how we have to reach out to our sister the earth, "because of the harm we have inflicted on her by our irresponsible use and abuse of the goods with which God has endowed her" (n 2). The pope points out how creation is different from nature, in so far as creation has to do with God's loving plan in which every creature has its own value and significance: ".... creation can only be understood as a gift from the outstretched hand of the Father of all, and as a reality illuminated by the love which calls us together into universal communion" (n 76).

The basic principle is the God-given dignity of the human person created in God's image and into whom God has breathed God's spirit and with whom God has entered into covenantal relationship. "Human dignity uniquely personal while grounded and realized in community, is the juncture at which the Christian message meets the world, and the world connects with the church," observes Christine Firer Hinze.[48] The Pastoral Constitution of the church in the Modern World (*Gaudium et Spes*)[49] describes this inter-connectedness in terms of solidarity (40-45). Solidarity is another name for love. The concluding paragraph of this lengthy document asserts: "Christians cannot yearn for anything more ardently than to serve the people of the modern world ever more generously and effectively." "By thus giving witness to the truth, we will share with others the mystery of the heavenly Father's love" (GS 93).

Jesus was God's good eye (*ayin tovah*) (Mt 6:22-23), looking out for the needs of others, and generous in giving to the poor, as opposed to *ayin raah* (to be self-centred).[50] This invites the church to have a generous heart for the world of our times, rather than to be preoccupied with its own identity. The shine of the church is its concern for society's vulnerable. "The more we read Jesus' words in their Hebraic setting, the more we discover that if we want to follow Jesus as his first Jewish disciples did, we need to learn to have a very "good eye.""[51]

The practice of love in service to fellow human beings is the exercise of mission. Love and communion presupposes otherness: otherness of persons, cultures, religions, contexts. If so the mission practice of love cannot be the same everywhere.

In some contexts it may imply giving rise to new communities, while in other contexts it may demand a new evangelization, yet in others dialogue between the followers of different religions or to make life more humane for those who go through the painful experience of dehumanization. Through all these the Christian community tries to follow the path (*halakah*) laid down by Jesus, the path of the reign of God. It is proclaiming the gospel of Jesus Christ. In the words of Pope Francis: "The church, guided by the Gospel of mercy and by love for mankind, hears the cry for justice and intends to respond to it with all her might" (EG 188). The church's call is "to be God's leaven in the midst of humanity" (EG 114), and in this all Christians participate, as "missionary disciples" (EG 120), with an inclusive attitude that is manifested in the genealogy of Jesus already.

Conclusion

Vatican II was a watershed event for mission, when it described the church as missionary by its very nature, as the continuation and expression of the divine love, divine reaching out. In a post-colonial and postmodern world this sense of reaching out in the spirit of love and service has to assume priority over being sent out. Biblically speaking, revelation and redemption began with creation and they are God's constant concern for creation, without any disruption or discontinuity. However, there was always the role of the few for the many, that climaxed in God's Messiah, Jesus, with his message of the divine reign, "the acceptable year of the Lord" (Lk 4:19). The community of his disciples continues that mission through its self-transcendence of reaching to the neighbour in love and service. The manner in which Jesus responded to the disciples of John the Baptist, regarding Jesus' identity as the Messiah, by referring to what was happening, rather than a direct affirmation that he was the

Messiah (Lk 7:22), suggests also that where ever that activity is continued, the Messiah is made present. That is the call of every Christian: to become God's presence, Emmanuel (Mt 1:23) by sacramentalising the love of God manifested in Jesus Christ.

Endnotes

[1] Not only most of the bishops participating in the Council were of western origin, but also the themes and language of the Council reflect the western church.

[2] The rise of the various subaltern theologies such as the Dalit Theology in India, the Theology of Struggle in the Philippines, the Minjung Theology in Korea, the Buraka Theology in Japan, The Asian Feminist Theology and others are all expressions of this rising consciousness of the little ones.

[3] Iosif L. Bosch, "Christian Mission Read in the Freedom of the Spirit," *International Review of Mission,* 397 (2013), 169.

[4] Ibid.

[5] Augustine, *The Literal Meaning of Genesis 1:36.* Augustine in *De Trinitate* dwells on the goodness of God (1.31), God as love (4.1), and the God's mission of sending the Son and the Spirit (2.5).

[6] Elizabeth A. Johnson, *Ask the Beasts: Darwin and the God of Love* (Bloomsbury: London, 2014), 140.

[7] Ibid.

[8] Ibid, 143.

[9] Diarmuid O'Mrchu, *Quantum Theology,* (New York: Crossroad, 2004), 46.

[10] Catherine La Cugna, *God For Us: The Trinity and Christian Life,* (San Francisco: Harper Collins, 1991), 250.

[11] Walter Kasper, *Mercy: The Essence of the Gospel and the Key to Christian Life,* (New York: Paulist Press, 2013), 48.

[12] Kasper, *Mercy,* 231.

[13] Ulrich Wilckens, *Theologie des Neuen Testaments,* 2/1 (Neukirchen-Vluyn: Neukirchner Ferlag, 2007), 93, in Kasper, 48.

[14] Lois Tverberg, *Walking in the Dust of Rabbi Jesus,* (Grand Rapids: Zondervan, 2012), 51 ff.

[15] Charles Darwin, *The Origin of Species,* (New York: Signet Classics, 2003), 459.

[16] See Denis Edwards, *Partaking of God: Trinity, Evolution and Ecology* (Collegeville, Minnesota: Michael Glazier, 2014), 75.

[17] Stephen Hawking, *A Brief History of Time. From the Big Bang to Black Holes* (New York: Bantam, 1988), 174.

[18] Denis Edwards, *Partaking of God*, 78.

[19] Dogmatic Constitution on Divine Revelation, **Dei Verbum,** Pope Paul VI, 1965, No 2: In His goodness and wisdom God chose to reveal Himself and to make known to us the hidden purpose of His will (see Eph. 1:9) by which through Christ, the Word made flesh, man might in the Holy Spirit have access to the Father and come to share in the divine nature (see Eph. 2:18; 2 Peter 1:4). Through this revelation, therefore, the invisible God (see Col. 1;15, 1 Tim. 1:17) out of the abundance of His love speaks to men as friends (see Ex. 33:11; John 15:14-15) and lives among them (see Bar. 3:38), so that He may invite and take them into fellowship with Himself. This plan of revelation is realized by deeds and words having an inner unity: the deeds wrought by God in the history of salvation manifest and confirm the teaching and realities signified by the words, while the words proclaim the deeds and clarify the mystery contained in them. By this revelation then, the deepest truth about God and the salvation of man shines out for our sake in Christ, who is both the mediator and the fullness of all revelation.

[20] Dean Fleming, *Recovering the Full Mission of God: A Biblical Perspective on Being, Doing and Telling,* (Downers Grove, Illinois: IVP Academic, 2013,118.

[21] Francis J. Moloney, *Love in the Gospel of John: An Exegetical, Theological, and Literary Study* (Grand Rapids, MI: Baker Academic, 2013), 100.

[22] Moloney, 136.

[23] Elizabeth Johnson, *Ask the Beasts: Darwin and the God of Love*, 199.

[24] Gerald O'Collins, *Interpreting Jesus* (London: Geoffrey Chapman, 1983), 51.

[25] Ibid.

[26] Walter Kasper, *The God of Jesus Christ,* trans. Matthew J. O'Connell (NY: Crossroad, 1986), 194.

[27] Denis Edwards, *Partaking of God: Trinity, Evolution and Ecology* (Collegeville, Minnesota: Michael Glazier, 2014), 37.

[28] Ibid, 38.

[29] Christopher Wright, *The Mission of God: Unlocking the Bible's Grand Narrative* (Nottingham: IVP, 2008), 25.

[30] Ibid, 29. As far as Vatican II is concerned, its very first insight was that mission is not an appendage of the church, but the very expression of its nature, derived from its origin, God's self-reaching out. Cf. E. Schillebeeckx, *Vatican II: The Real Achievement,* (London: Sheed & Ward, 1967), 44-45. Mission is the hermeneutical key to understand the Council.

[31] Ross S. Blackburn, *The God who Makes Himself Known: The Missionary Heart of the book of Exodus*, (Downers Grove, IL: Intervarsity Press, 2012), 83-112.

[32] Robert Alter, *The Art of Biblical Narrative* (Berkeley: Harper Collins, 1981), 158.

[33] Dennis Hart, "Pentecostal Letter to Youth," *Kairos* 25 (8 June 2014): 22.

[34] Pope Francis, "Address to the Major Religious Superiors," November 7, 2014. (http://www.vatican.va/content/francesco/it/speeches/2014/November/documents/papa-francesco_20141107. accessed on 24-12-2014.

[35] *Letter to Diognetus*, 6.

[36] Walter Kasper, *Mercy*, 168.

[37] Walter Kasper, *Mercy*, 169.

[38] "Archbishop calls for a "Reality Check," bbc.com/news/world-europe-32862824. Accessed on 24-5-2015.

[39] Mary Motte, "A Roman Catholic Perspective on Missiological Education," in *Missiological Education for the 21ˢᵗ Century*, J Dudley Woodberry, Charles Van Engen and Edgar Elliston (eds) (New York: Orbis Books, 1997), 77.

[40] Ibid.

[41] Abraham J Heschel, *Man is not alone: A Philosophy of Religion*, (New York: Farar, Straus and Young, 1951), 43, quoted in *Abraham Joshua Heschel: The Call of Transcendence*, Shai Held (ed), Bloomington: Indiana University Press, 2013, 9.

[42] Ross Langmead, *The Word Made Flesh: Towards an Incarnational Missiology*, (Maryland: University Press of America, 2004), 20.

[43] *Ad Gentes* anchored the missionary nature of the church on the very missionary nature of God, by stating that it flows from "that fountain of love." (AG 2).

[44] Julian of Norwich, *Showings*, (Mahwah: Paulist Press, 1978), 299 in James Boyce, *Born Bad*, (Collingwood, Vic, 2014), 47.

[45] Pope Francis, "Address to the Meeting of the Congregation for Bishops," 27 February 2014, n6.

[46] Karl Rahner, "How to receive a Sacrament and Mean it," *The Sacraments: Readings in Contemporary Sacramental Theology*, (ed) Michael J Taylor (New York: Alba House, 1981),74, quoted in Vincent Donovan, *The Church in the Midst of Creation* (New York: Orbis Books, 1989), 64.

[47] Benedict XVI, Address to the Brazilian Bishops in the Cathedral of Sao Paulo, Brazil (11 May 2007), see EG 48.

[48] Christine Firer Hinze, "Straining toward Solidarity in a Suffering World," in *Vatican II Forty Years Later*, Eilliam Madger (ed) (New York: Orbis Books, 2005), 170.

[49] *Gaudium et Spes*, a key document of the Council, had its origin on the floor of the Council following Cardinal Leon-Joseph Suenens' historic intervention on December 4, 1962 arguing for a central vision for the council that should concern the church's identity *ad intra* as well as its service to the world, *ad extra*. See *The Documents of Vatican II*, Walter M Abbot (ed) (New York: Guild Press, 1966), 184.

[50] Lois Tverberg, *Walking in the Dust of Rabbi Jesus*, 69-79.

[51] Tverberg, *Walking in the Dust of Rabbi Jesus*, 79.

Mission at the Crossroads of Humanization of Life

Biblical and Magisterial Perspectives

The church, the community of disciples the Lord Jesus committed to continue his mission, finds that every new day is a challenge for forty percent of its sisters and brothers of the world population with inadequate food and shelter, with no health care systems, not knowing how to read and write, and not having an employment to earn a living, and with little prospects of improving their harrowing situations of dehumanization, humiliation and shame. This is aggravated by a process of awareness building that has filtered down through the bottom of most societies due to various technological developments and communication and this, in turn, makes the existing conditions doubly unbearable, frequently leading to frustration and acts of violence like the Maoist movement, in India.

The relation between humanization of life and mission has been a moot point of discussion in missiological circles since the second part of the 20th century, even though works of charity have always been considered integral to Christian practice. The Christian social tradition is a tradition of thinking and acting, as the manifestation of the ethical intuition and commitment to the gospel. Understanding of the Christian mystery that inspires social commitment has attracted deeper reverence from the majority of Christians since the end of the 19th century. According to the North American theologian Frederick Herzog, this expresses God's closeness to history.[1]

The present age is experiencing the need to build up a just and fraternal world and it is looking for a better understanding of the complex problems of development and social justice and the way the world is functioning. The community of the disciples of the Lord Jesus needs biblically based theological principles to guide it in its search for the link between development and social justice.

What this chapter tries to present is a firm scripturally based framework for development without the spiritual/physical wedge that normally bedevils theologizing. It will be shown how the Bible, both the Old and New Testaments, does advocate a transformational development. Eventually it will be argued that the Christian mission is a manifesting of the transformational development[2] with its relational emphasis accruing from the kingdom ministry of Jesus Christ, as the manifestation of the transforming power of God. Though the chapter presumes a wider readership, it is written from a Catholic experience and relying on the Catholic social teachings.

Development is concerned with human beings and social systems so that they can organize their activities to satisfy their basic needs and non-material wants like education, knowledge, spiritual fulfilment and others keeping with the basic human dignity,[3] leading to the reduction of poverty, unemployment and inequality. Obviously, it is not only a question of income generation, but the quality of life as human persons with freedom of choice to determine the course of one's life, with self-respect, triggering happiness.[4]

Transformational Development is different from Developmentalism that was in vogue in the post-World War II days. The success of the US economy created a euphoria leading to the presumption that economic growth was the key to the solution of poverty. US model economic development was recommended to all the poor countries across the world with the presumption that if the third world countries abandoned their agricultural societies and industrialized, their expanded gross national product and the subsequent improved status in international trade would relieve them of their national poverty. However, this whole developmental theory did not take into account how the US and other major powers, through the Marshall Plan, gained access to trade relations with Africa and South America, who held colonial ties to major European countries in exchange for aid to Europe for post-war reconstruction. This in turn removed the natural resources from the poorer nations to the richer nations.

The "new economy" of development theory developed "centres" or richer economies and "periphery" or dependent economies", observes Judith Merkle.[5] The resources, balance of trade and brain power were monopolized in a dependency relationship with the first world, ending development, with increased poverty. This, along with the conviction that some nations are poor, not because they failed to develop, but because they have been prevented by others from doing so, and the conviction how large segments of populations are excluded from active participation in shaping the social economic, and political structures, have popularized the terminology of liberation over development. This is further affirmed by the impact of liberation theology that seeks to bring the gospel to the concrete struggle to human liberation and social transformation. Poverty is not just a question of underdevelopment or the fruit of laziness; rather it is the result of a well laid out social system, though unjust, with its vice-like grip.

Today all would agree that no civilized people can feel satisfied when a section of their fellow humans exist in conditions of such absolute human misery, and this is reflected in the emphasis every religion places on the importance of working for the alleviation of poverty and inequality.

Biblical Perspectives Old Testament

The biblical revelation begins with God's self-manifestation in relation to the dehumanized situation of a people (Ex 3:6-7). Later, due to their unfaithfulness, Israel suffers exile from which they are restored to their land under the Persian Emperor Cyrus. When we examine the prophetic literature, we see how the all-important theme is that of justice towards the poor (Is 58:6-7; Jer 9:24; Hos 2: 19; Amos 4:1; 5:24; Mic 6:8). The God of the Bible is a God of justice, bringing peace through justice in so far as it is distributive justice that seeks all to have enough to live. God is just because God stood against the Egyptian empire to save some doomed slaves. God prefers justice to injustice, righteousness to unrighteousness, and therefore God is liberator.

This ancient Jewish tradition was destined to clash with the Roman commercialization, urbanization and monetization in the first century Jewish homeland.[6]

For ancient Near Eastern peoples, land played a key role in their lives.

"We can see a tension within the attitudes towards land tenure in the ancient Near East. On the one hand, there was the recognition that land was a unique resource that must receive special regulation in order to prevent the ruin of the people. On the other hand, there was a movement toward greater individual freedom in the use and disposal of the land, allowing for the possibility of latifundism (agribusiness) and the pauperization of masses of people. It appears that the ancient Near East was pulled in the latter direction, and it was in such a context in which Israel came into being."[7]

Generally, all ancient people had the sense that land is divine gift to people even as in modern times in 2010 the then Australian Prime Minister Kevin Rudd wanted to impose 40% tax on the profit of the mining companies with the argument that the resources in the land belonged to the people. Similar understanding could have been the background of the Jubilee legislation enshrined in Leviticus 25. The logic behind divine justice is human equality, radical egalitarianism that manifests in specific laws. Inequality among God's people is insistently shown to be against the justice of God. God is against indebtedness, control, enslavement and dispossession. Equality and egalitarianism are constitutive of biblical thinking. The core message of the Old Testament is that "Israel's God is the one true God of all the earth and all nations because this God alone is a God of justice and righteousness for those systematically vulnerable, for the weak, the orphan, the lonely, the destitute and the needy," writes Crossan.[8]

Though Israel was restored to its own land from exile in Babylonia, it continued to experience suffering under foreign overlords, a suffering interpreted as punishment for Israel's sins. Hence the promise of forgiveness, spoken by the exilic prophets like Isaiah, Jeremiah and Ezekiel, continued to ignite the mind of Israel, making the post-exilic prophets speak of the liberation still to be completed.[9] They described this liberation employing the language of the return from exile: the new exodus. It is against this background that Jesus announced that God's reign is at hand (Mk 1:14) - the very centre of his mission.

Jesus' Ministry

The coming of the Kingdom of God was not a matter of abstract ideas or timeless truths or a sort of new religion, a doctrine or a soteriology, but was the pinnacle of Israel's story and its climax, its decisive moment.[10] However, at the same time Jesus was gripped by a strong sense of vocation from God whom he experienced as "Abba", implying a specific role as the son. In this sense his mission was manifesting the Father (Jn 12:45; 14:9). Through all that he did and said, Jesus not only manifested God but also showed how God's reign was breaking in and through him, through his ministry.

At the time of a tense and unstable political situation in Palestine under the Roman rule and in the context of Galilee becoming more urban and cosmopolitan, there was a crisis of culture and uncertainty. The Roman rule made life for the Jews the antithesis of everything they believed about themselves and their relationship with God. The imperial Roman theology claimed the emperor as god and Roman culture as the unifying element of the empire. At this time of change and crisis, hopes about God's reign and God's messiah were high. The Jesus movement was in sharp contrast to the Roman urbanization that dislocated the common rural folk, pushing them from poverty to destitution. Jesus' primary focus was on peasants dispossessed by Roman commercialization and Herodian urbanization in the late 20s in lower Galilee.[11]

The coming of the Messiah as presented by the gospels was radically different from the way people had understood God and God's ways. God does not come in clouds of glory, but in a way unimportant and unrecognized. Even Jesus' own family does not understand what is happening (Mk 3:21). At about 30 years of age, he left his work and his family and inspired a group of people that was willing to leave everything and journey with him. He wandered the countryside for about one to three years preaching, teaching, and healing. The central point was that God's reign has broken into history through him and in him. This he manifested in the most unconventional ways: he touched the untouchables and he stood against systemic injustice, particularly that of the religious institutions; he showed that God is not pleased by the blind following of laws of rituals and ritual purity, but by entering into the lives of the victims of these laws, whom he characterized as the little ones: the blind, the lame, the leprosy-affected, the elderly, those with bodily oozing, those who knew nothing of the law, the poor, those who mourn, hunger, the persecuted, widows, ... the list goes on. Through all these he showed how the divine reign, foretold and passionately hoped for by the prophets, was manifesting itself. It is a time when the oppressed go free, when those who are bound are set at liberty, when the blind receive sight. He showed through his ministry how the Kingdom would look and how his followers could associate themselves with him in this work by reversing the situations of those who mourn, who hunger, and so on.

The Matthean beatitudes have been traditionally spiritualized to encourage the poor and suffering to continue in their dehumanized situation, but promising a spiritual reward! Warren Carter, however, has convincingly argued that the Matthean gospel is a counter-narrative, standing over against the status quo of the domineering imperial power and synagogue control.[12] In this vision, the first part of the beatitudes (Mt 5: 3-6) refers to righteousness and the oppressive situations of distress which God's reign will reverse as shown in the second part (vs. 7-10). The first part critiques the political, economic, social, religious and personal distress that results from the powerful elite, who enrich their own position at the expense of the poor who mourn and hunger for righteousness, who are meek because they are helpless. The remaining four beatitudes are concerned with human actions to reverse the situation of the poor. Through the human actions of compassion, mercy, justice, and disinterested service, God manifests God's reign; they enact God's purposes for just societal relations. Thus, the poor will experience the coming of the Kingdom.[13]

The Lucan Manifesto

The Lucan inaugural proclamation of Jesus (4:18-19) is considered to be a sort of manifesto of Jesus. It is linked with the great Jubilee year that is described in Leviticus 25:10-17 in so far as the text Jesus quoted, Isaiah 61:1-2, was the synagogue reading for the celebration of the Jubilee. By quoting this very passage Jesus is claiming how the Jubilee, the acceptable year of the Lord, has come in him. The Jubilee was good news to the poor in so far as the main ingredients of Jubilee were the return of the land as well as freeing the slaves and giving them sufficient means of livelihood. The poor benefited by the arrival of Jubilee. It was a divine revolution to retrieve the original equality and fraternity, which the Israelites enjoyed when all had their own fig trees and vineyard (1King 4:25), a symbolic expression of social and economic well-being. Due to human weakness this ideal situation could be destroyed. However, Yahweh did not want such an unnatural situation to continue endlessly and hence we have the Jubilee prescription.

At the time of Jesus, the poor, the blind, the lame, the bonded, were eking out a dehumanizing existence in so far as they had to beg for their livelihood- they were not considered to be fully human. Jesus not only quoted Isaiah but systematically carried out his claim of ushering in the year of the Lord, through his healings and other symbolic gestures like the oft-repeated all-inclusive table fellowship, thereby manifesting that the poor of any sort are restored to their human dignity and reinstated into the society. The many table-fellowships of Jesus described in the gospels, in the words of G S Key "are not only a well-known, historically certain feature of his ministry, but a highly significant feature as well."[14] Dominic Crossan, one of the best of the **Historical Jesus** scholars, upholds open commensality as a leading aspect of Jesus' ministry. Crossan writes: "Open commensality is the symbol and embodiment of radical egalitarianism, of an absolute equality of people that denies the validity of any discrimination between them and negates the necessity of any hierarchy among them."[15] Joachim Jeremias too writes about the significance of the frequently held Table Fellowships of the Lord: "They are an expression of the mission and message of Jesus (Mk 2:17), eschatological meals, anticipatory celebrations of the feast in the end time

(Mt 8:11 par.), in which the community of saints is already being represented (Mk 2:19). The inclusion of sinners in the community of salvation, achieved in the table fellowship, is the most meaningful expression of the message of the redeeming love of God."[16]

Even the Johannine gospel, the object of frequent spiritualization by commentators, has to be understood from this perspective of justice and righteousness to the poor. The key text used for the spiritual understanding of John is 3:16: "God so loved the world ... whoever believes in him should not perish but have eternal life." However, this verse is to be read along with the following verses, more so v.20: "For all who do evil hate the light, and do not come to the light, lest their deeds should be exposed. But those who do what is true come to the light, that it may be clearly seen that their deeds have been wrought in God." It is an engagement with the world choosing deeds of light over those of evil. It is a question of how one responds to people and structures that are dark, evil and bring death to the world.

Jesus not only cures the leprosy-affected person but also makes sure that he is re-instated into the society (Mk 1:44). He does not allow human relationships to be derailed due to sickness or bodily situations. His ministry was the definitive divine revolution of recapturing the original equality and acceptance, a society without discrimination and hierarchy.

Human Centred Ministry

From what has been said so far it is already clear how the ministry of Jesus was centred on human beings. In fact the very Incarnation, the single most important aspect of Christianity, was the affirmation of the human person, for as the Second

Vatican Council document *Gaudium et Spes* insisted, through his Incarnation Jesus united himself with every human being (GS 22), with whom, I would suggest, he was united already at the moment of creation. Hence, the Incarnation is the affirmation of the glory and dignity of the human person. Donal Dorr has argued how the title "Son of Man" has actually to be translated as 'the Human One' (*ho huios tou antropou*) which in turn, is the affirmation of the humanity that Jesus shared with every single individual. Donal Dorr goes on to say: "The title may even hint that Jesus is 'THE human' – one who is the epitome of humanity."[17] Thus, Jesus is the representative and fulfilment of humanity's aspirations. Not only what Jesus was, but also all that he did, point to how humans are to live a full human life with all its glory and dignity.

Jesus' oft-repeated breaking of the Sabbath laws is in fact a relativising of the Divine in terms of the human person. For the Jews the Sabbath rules could not be broken since they were given by God the Absolute. But Jesus' standard attitude is, the Sabbath is made for human beings, for their well-being. (Mk 2:27).

Similarly, the purity pollution laws too are to be seen in the context of the significance of the human person. Jesus touched women (Mk 1:21), touched leprosy-affected people (Mk 1:41), called the polluted and polluting woman who touched him, "My daughter," (Mk 5:34), defended the woman caught in adultery (Jn 8:3-11), accepted the hospitality of a tax collector (Lk 19:1f.), and so on.

Jesus showed how the way to God is through the neighbour (Mt 25:31-46). In fact, as far as the final judgment is concerned the way we treat the neighbour is the only thing that counts. The Christian specificity is this concern for the human person, the neighbour, anyone who is wounded in any way (Lk 25:30-37). Restoring the dignity of the human person was his mission manifesto as we saw; it is his very identity as the Messiah (Lk 7:22-23).

Daniel Groody draws attention to how Jesus, by becoming a Galilean, identifies himself with a rejected group so that he can reveal the lie of the world that degrades human beings.[18] Jesus showed how the reign of God is the radical inclusion of all, by welcoming all, especially those whom the world of his time rejected (Lk 14:13-14). A sector that he showed special concern for, was that of the women in the society. The typical outlook on women at the time of Jesus is manifested in the Jewish males' thanksgiving that God had not made them women![19]

At the time of Jesus, the wife was considered to be her husband's property and disadvantaged in many ways.[20] Yet Jesus, contrary to the prevailing presumption, pronounces how a man can also commit adultery against his wife, and this was revolutionary (Mt 19:9). We have already spoken of the compassionate way Jesus treated women.

Jesus was speaking in terms of the Jewish hopes of the times, viz., Israel's God is ushering in God's reign, which affects the entire world in its space and time.[21] Wright elsewhere shows how, when the Jews looked forward to the coming of God's Kingdom, they did not think of the end of the space-time world, but rather that God is going to act dramatically within the space-time world, as he had done at the time of the Exodus.[22] Jesus was showing how divine reality is breaking into their midst, doing what they have been longing for, through his very presence and ministry.

Further, the use of the Kingdom symbol did not always imply a resurrection or life after death insofar as Israel's basic world view did not imply them. Hence the priority of making the salvation of souls the aim of our mission cannot be fully justified. This does not mean a rejection of the latter; it only reminds us of how mission has to be integral as Jesus' mission was, culminating in his resurrection, manifested also in his promise to the thief at his right on the cross, "Today you shall be with me in paradise" (Lk 23:43), a salvation that Jesus describes elsewhere as having come already due to a changed life and social outlook (Lk19:9).

Jesus not only taught about the Kingdom, but enacted it in his own life and ministry through symbolic acts like the table-fellowships, dealings with women, healings, forgiving, feeding, casting out demons, etc. Through these symbolic deeds and teachings he was not only presenting a new vision of the Kingdom, but at the same time challenging other visions of the Kingdom like those of the Pharisees, and Essenes. In contrast to the traditional expectations of the Kingdom as a time of perfect adherence to the cultic rules (Sadducees), or the meticulous observance of the law (Pharisees), or the following of the monastic life of the Qumran community (Essenes), or a radical direct divine intervention (Apocalyptic hopes) or a violent revolution (Zealots), Jesus showed that the Kingdom is a matter of radical love and communion. When others saw God's forgiveness in terms of the temple and cult, for Jesus it was welcoming the sinner, dining with them, accepting the unacceptable and unconditional forgiveness like that of the prodigal father. In Jesus God celebrates all that God has been and is. As Diarmuid O'Murchu has underlined, the divine involvement with humans that started six million years ago when the first humans appeared on the face of the earth and with that human salvation as well, reaches its fulfilment in Jesus Christ.[23]

Kingdom and Salvation

Although we have already discussed the Kingdom in the context of the Jewish expectations, we still need to speak about the traditional understanding of salvation associated with Jesus' ministry, and more so with his death and resurrection.

Redemption was the central concept of Israel's religion and life. Beginning with Exodus 6:6 there is an overwhelming understanding of the divine restoration, reflected in various biblical texts. The idea of redemption is reflected in no less than 150 verses of the bible.[24] This in turn makes the eschatological hope of YHWH's saving intervention or visitation the focus of Israel's faith, in the context of the lived experience of evil, represented by foreign rule. For Israel what was important was their understanding of redemption as an existence of original equality and fraternity and well-being described in I Kings 4: The prophecies made in the context of the deportations and exile, to console the people, lead to the hope of a future Messiah – redeemer. He need not have been a divine person; in fact, Cyrus is described as a redeemer in Isaiah 45.1.

The three central aspects of the traditional hopes were the return from exile, the defeat of evil represented by foreign rule, and the return of YHWH to Zion. These Jesus applied to himself through his prophetic Kingdom announcement.[25] The long night of exile, the present evil age would give way to the dawn of renewal and restoration, the age to come. This hope was associated with the royal settings, the king who would come would be the agent through whom YHWH would accomplish this great renewal (Zech 1:8). This royal connotation had links also with the Temple as the central theme as exemplified by David, Solomon, Hezekiah and Josiah. Judas Maccabaeus gave rise to a priestly and royal dynasty by cleansing the temple. "Temple and kingship went hand in hand," points out Wright.[26]Jesus' triumphal entry into Jerusalem, riding on a donkey, and his actions in the temple, constituted the messianic praxis. John Meier writes: "Jesus' entry into Jerusalem and the cleansing of the temple constituted a messianic demonstration, a messianic critique, a messianic fulfilment event, and a sign of the messianic restoration of Israel."[27] This in turn alarmed the chief priests who ruled the temple and thus the Jewish religion and nation indirectly. Jesus' symbolic action spoke unmistakably to the priests who were well-versed in texts like Zechariah 9.9f. The first century mainstream Jewish leaders, the self-styled guardians of the Jewish faith, decided to eliminate him and they did it with the help of the Roman administration. The ministry of the Lord culminates on the cross. However the God who affirmed him to be God's Son and thus affirmed his ministry at the time of the baptism at Jordan (Mk 1:11) and at the time of the transfiguration on a high mountain (Mk 9:7), now intervenes and raises him up and thus definitively affirming him and his ministry (Acts 2:22-24).

The disciples who had abandoned him at the crucifixion regroup themselves in the light of their Easter experience. Easter is the key to the recognition of Jesus as the Messiah. However, this recognition raises the question of how the Messiah could die on the cross, a curse according to Deuteronomy (21:22). Hence, we come across the explanation why Jesus died for our sins; he became a curse for us (1Cor 15:3; Gal 3:13) to fulfil the scriptures.

Though according to the gospels, the incarnation took place as part of the divine plan, rooted in God's love and Jesus' being put to death, in Neil Ormerod's words, it "was the result of a fairly grubby story of power and politics, of enemies and rivalries, of people who very early in the ministry of Jesus set out to destroy him, discrediting his teaching and his mission (Mark 3:6),"[28] scripture scholars interpreted Pauline writings as an act of atonement (Rom 3:25), a justifying act (Rom 5:9). This has been further buttressed by the "cup of blood ... sign of forgiveness" (Mt 26:28). However, as Dominic Crossan and Jonathan L. Reed have pointed out, for Paul divine righteousness refers to distribution and not retribution. God's justice is God's righteousness. God does what is just by doing what is right. God *is* justice, i.e., righteousness, it is the very character of God.[29] Crossan and Reed argue the modern confusion regarding justification arises due to a wrong interpretation of justice, i.e., rather than seeing it as distributive, seen as retributive, based on the modern law courts. In the Hebrew Scriptures the primary and basic meaning of God's justice is distributive. When justice is done by humans by distribution, retribution follows.[30]

Similarly, the cup of forgiveness is to be understood in the context of forgiveness in the gospels. As N.T. Wright has stressed, forgiveness is the sign of the return of YHWH, the eschatological times. Through the cup Jesus asserts it is already now.[31] The gospels attribute Jesus' conflict with the authorities to his human-centred interpretation of the law, his forgiving sins, and his attack on the temple and the authorities, and these in turn precipitate his arrest and execution. The subsequent theological reflection to a large extent focused on the images contained in the Pauline writings. Tertullian (.ca.160) developed the notion of ransom.[32] Gregory of Nazianzus questioned this motive of ransom, but Gregory of Nyssa justified it by saying it was a sort of deceiving the devil! Origin made it a sacrifice, prompting God to grant propitiation and pardon for sins.[33] Today, as N.T. Wright insists, by and large scripture scholars like Meier, Sanders, Chilton, Crossan and others would link Jesus' death with the Kingdom proclamation and his action in the temple.[34] If at all we want to talk about the salvation from sin that Jesus brought about is that of the overcoming of selfishness. It is a transition from self-centeredness to other centeredness. Selfishness is the root of all sin that we come across everywhere, including among Christians.

Social Teaching of the Catholic Church

The modern social teachings of the Catholic church were occasioned by the deplorable conditions of the poor in the wake of the industrial revolution and the emergence of capitalism that forced the church to search for justice as a fresh expression of its own mission and service to the world. The enormous human suffering resulting from the unresolved issues of industrialization and the rise of socialism and communism challenged the church to play a proactive role, leading to Pope Leo XIII's encyclical, *Rerum Novarum* (New Order of Things) of 1891. The encyclical led the way to the new concept of "social justice" where justice is applied to structural questions such as the relationship between capital and labour, the family, the state, equality and inequality, and ownership.[35] The encyclical deplored the conditions of the working class where "a very few rich and exceedingly rich men have laid a yoke almost of slavery on the unnumbered masses of non-owning workers" (RN 6) and argued for the workers' right for a living wage for a family rather than a wage determined by the law of supply and demand and pleaded for healthy working conditions.

Rerum Novarum became a trail-blazer for a series of teachings on the social mission of the church from the Catholic Magisterium. On the fortieth anniversary of RN, Pope Pius XI came out with another equally powerful encyclical, *Quadragesimo anno* (Fortieth Year), occasioned by the Great Depression, the consolidation of the Russian Revolution and the emergence of fascist dictatorships in Italy and Germany. The Pope emphasized the centrality of human dignity as the basis of all human rights. Pius XI argued that all must receive their due share in the distribution of created goods according to the demands of common good and social justice (QA n 58).

Both RN and QA were concerned with the conditions of workers and the poor in the *first* world. This was rectified by Pope John XXIII in his encyclical *Mater et Magistra* (Mother and Teacher) (1961). The Pope extended the notion of welfare for the poor beyond the capitalist system, and internationalized the Catholic social teaching saying: "Perhaps the most pressing question of our day concerns the relationship between economically advanced commonwealths and those that are in process of development. The former enjoys the conveniences of life; the latter experience dire poverty" (MM n 157). John XXIII's *Pacem in Terris* (Peace on Earth), 1963, outlined new avenues of social justice in light of major changes across the globe. The Pope recognized freedom and human rights as the foundation of the social order.

John XXIII's approach is continued in the Ecumenical Council, Vatican II, that he convoked. Of all the decrees and declarations of the Council *Gaudium et Spes* (Pastoral Constitution on Church), deserves special mention as it captures the Council's approach to the poor and marginalized of the world. The very opening words speak volumes: "The joys and hopes, the griefs and anxieties of the people of this age, especially those who are poor or in any way afflicted, those too are the joys and hopes, the griefs and anxieties of the followers of Christ." GS warmly welcomes modern human longing for dignity, brotherhood, participation, freedom and equality. It encourages the social movements that embody those legitimate aspirations (n 41). God intended the earth and all that it contains for the use of every human being and people. "If a person is in extreme necessity, that person has the right to take from the riches of others what that person needs," and exhorts all individuals and governments to "Feed the people dying of hunger, because if you have not fed them you have killed them" (n 69). There cannot be true peace without a just economic world order. The distinctive contribution of Vatican II was the way in which it brought the whole social ministry to the centre of the Catholic church's mission through the Pastoral Constitution, *Gaudium et Spes.*

Populorum Progressio (On the Development of Peoples) 1967, Pope Paul VI's social encyclical, refers to the "political pressure and economic domination, aimed at maintaining or acquiring control of a few" (n 57). Integral human development, a development of the whole person and of all persons and peoples is a guide towards social action. The importance of basic education and literacy is the key that enables people to assume responsibility for themselves, their lives and their world. Paul VI constituted the social wing of the Catholic church, the Pontifical Commission of Justice and Peace. The Synod of Bishops 1971, declared how action on behalf of justice and participation in the transformation of the world is constitutive of the church's mission. In the encyclical *Octogesmo Adveniens* (A Call to Action) 1971, Paul VI recognized clearly the significance of political activity for solving economic and social problems (OA n 50).

John Paul II in the encyclical *Laborem Exercens* (On Human Work) 1981, affirmed the priority of labour over capital and called for respect for human subjectivity and the dignity of the human person in the organization of labour and production.

In *Sollicitudo Rei Socialis* (On Social Concern) 1987, John Paul called for solidarity as a remedy for the growing isolation of people from ties that would generate concern for the neighbour. Community formed through solidarity is related to sustainable development. Good society is not only a growing domestic product but includes also a better quality of family life and friendship, satisfaction with work, more leisure and a sense of spiritual richness. John Paul II called for a moral understanding of development that includes the trajectory of human growth toward otherness and depth that is inherent in the Catholic social tradition (SRS 28). The Pope reiterated his call for a change of lifestyles, of models of production and consumption, and of the established structures of power which govern societies, in his encyclical *Centesimus Annus* (Hundredth Year) 1991.

The social teaching of the church is not just a listing of principles for social action, nor strategies to solve problems of poverty, welfare, environment, globalization and others, nor even the social action itself as shown in the service of Pope Francis. Ever since he took the reins of the pastoral care of the Catholic Church, he aligned himself with the forces affirming the dignity of the human person in word and deed. His visiting the central prison in Rome on Holy Thursday to wash the feet of the prisoners, including a Muslim woman, or his going to the asylum seekers' camp and offering hospitality to some of them within the Vatican, or providing space for shower and toilet facilities for the poor within the Vatican, are only some of the examples of his tireless reaching out to the dehumanized.

Social mission could be described as the church's effort to provide a systematic normative theory and practice in relation to the social vision of the faith to the concrete conditions in which faith is lived. "It is an act of the church in context," comments Judith Merkle.[36]

The Social Mission of the Church

In continuation with the Jewish apocalyptic vision, the primitive community saw the resurrection of Christ as ushering in the "new age", the celestial world completely ruled by God, already now, as opposed to "this age" which is sin-dominated. The full manifestation of the new age would take place at the second coming of Christ, and it was expected to be imminent. However, with the transition from the primitive community to the early community, we see the Hellenistic worldview gradually mingling with the apocalyptic vision. The Hellenistic worldview contained another dualism: that of the world of the senses and that of true understanding, the intelligible world. Through his ascension to the spiritual world, Jesus Christ becomes the mediator between the spiritual and the sensible worlds. The whole theology of victory over death is developed in the context of the Hellenistic dualism, of the world of the senses and of the spiritual, the world of matter as opposed to the transcendent world. Whereas Jesus brought a salvation connected with life on earth, now it is transferred to the other world! Hence, we can speak of the need to retrieve the prophetic ministry of the Lord that was affirmed by his resurrection.

The prophetic service of the church is the logical sequence to its call and mandate to follow its Lord, who identified himself as a prophet (Mk 6:4, Mt 13:57; Lk 4.24). The church has to judge itself by the content of its ministry rather than the content of its doctrinal claims. It is not primarily the cult and the institution that makes the church what it is, but its continuation of the ministry of its Lord. It has to draw inspiration from the life and ministry of the Jesus of history and has to identify itself with the cause for which he was killed and was raised again. We have seen how he had neither time nor interest in moving among the religious leaders of the time whose only concern was their own belly and their image. In fact, his strongest woes are pronounced against them (Mt 23:13ff). He was by contrast in constant fellowship with the little ones and the "no-people", weighed down by the burdens imposed upon them by the religious rulers.

At the heart of the whole theology of involvement in development is the Christian faith in the truth that humans are created in the image of God and God has entered into a covenant relationship with all human beings. This human dignity calls for certain rights and freedoms that enable humans to live as humans. In other words, the mystery of humans cannot be understood without the mystery of God.

The church exists above all to be at the service of the poor and the victims of society, so that they can experience the fruits of the arrival of the acceptable year of the Lord (Luke 4:19). Wherever and whenever artificial dependency is created in the socio-economic or even in religious fields for the benefit of the powerful, it generates dehumanization. This is compounded by laws of ritual pollution or laws that segregate sectors of humanity as permanently impure as in the case of the caste system in India. This has no logical basis but is a sheer figment of the mind. Though God created the victims of imposed ritual impurity in God's own image (Gen 1:26), this image is irrecognizably disfigured in them due to the inhuman treatments which they have to endure. The urgent need of any "God-talk" today is the recovery of human dignity for these people.

Commenting on Jesus' association with the outcasts, Roger Haight argues: "It seems fairly certain that Jesus directed his attention to people who stood outside the margins of society, and that this was a disturbing factor in his ministry and message for the religiously upright."[37] We saw how Jesus, through his association with sinners and tax collectors, became the externalization of the divine in rapport with the human. God's action in history is primarily manifested through his involvement with those on the margins and the dehumanized.

If Jesus' main concern was saving people from alienation, marginalization, and negation and to restore them to wholeness, the church's route should not be any different. Jesus needs followers for the mediation of God's compassionate love to all who suffer, all those who are oppressed, all those who are forced to the margins. That is the project that he has bequeathed to the community of his disciples in the world, God's plan for history.

Jesus' mission is to be read in the context in which we live, in which human suffering and marginalization are crystallized into forms of oppression imposed by human beings on other innocent human beings. Human suffering has to become the focus of church's service today. This, as Roger Haight rightly emphasizes, is "not because Christology will bear messianic solution to these problems, but because Jesus cannot be the Christ and salvation cannot be real without having some bearing on this situation."[38] The God manifested in his ministry is not a god who is inviolable, but the God ready to go through violation for the sake of the least and the lost. *Antodaya* (the rise of the least) is God's concern. We saw how this concern prompted Jesus to by-pass laws regarding the Sabbath and purity-pollution. Moving in the same spirit, mission today has to be moulded in the experience of people.

What are to be dismantled today are not so much religious differences as it was thought in the past, but the disgusting structures of dehumanization. These structures made Antony Raj, an Indian Dalit theologian write: "I feel that it is better for us Dalits to die on our feet than live on our knees before insolent men."[39] Jesus, through his ministry of identification with the poor and challenge of the structures that keep them dehumanized, sets into motion the resistive forces that seek to challenge the social, cultural, economic and religious structures today.

"What do you want me to do for you?" (Mt 20:32), Jesus asked the blind man. The dehumanized and marginalized poor of today are asking the church: that we may see, so that we can live as human beings, accepted and respected as such; that we may have equal opportunities. It is the blindness of the powerful of the society that condemns these to lead lives bereft of human dignity. The church's mission today above all is in this sphere of human existence. The poor want a share in decision-making so that they can benefit from the fruit of their labour and the product of their creativity.

If mission today does not take up the cry of the poor for the recovery of their lost human dignity and restore justice to them, it is empty of the Christian content that Jesus in his ministry had so much insisted upon. He is not concerned with the mediocre solutions of following the letter of the law but appeals to the generous depth of the human spirit, as we see in the case of the rehabilitation of the woman caught in adultery (Jn 8:3-11).

Our mission must be ruled by the methodological orientations of Jesus Christ whose tireless concern for individuals left him with little time to eat or sleep (Jn 4: 7 ff). He spares no words over the arrogance of the official religious powers that had little regard for individuals (Mt 23:13ff). The church, collectively and as individuals, must renounce making use of power for crippling others, or instrumentalizing and dehumanizing others. This could mean, for instance, religious and ecclesiastical authorities would not use power for subjugating the members of their congregation, but only to serve them (Mk 9:35). The gospel should never become a power for domination and marginalization.

The prophetic hermeneutic of the gospel in our times cannot tolerate any exploitative, divisive or oppressive force. The poor of our time must feel that the God of the Bible is with them and has heard their cry and seen their affliction (Ex 3:7ff), through the creation of an egalitarian and participative society. Informed by the vision of the Jesus of the gospels, the community of his disciples must come to the aid of people who need to be helped. The basic objective of mission is not the future of Christianity or the church, but the future of humankind as a whole plus that of planet Earth that has come to be victimized as merely a resource to be plundered as much as possible to satisfy the greed and pleasure of the relatively few who can afford it. The earth, of which we are an integral part, also shares the lot of the disfigured and exploited poor, crying for recognition and restoration.

The social fabric of modern humanity is interwoven from two realms of existence: politics and religions. We must collaborate with both. A real concern and genuine care for the weak, the poor and the oppressed cannot be achieved fully without associating ourselves with political life; the empowerment of the weak and dispossessed cannot be attained without political collaboration. Today we need a sort of political spirituality as exemplified by Mahatma Gandhi. In his first letter, Peter instructs Christians always to give an account of the hope that is in them (3:15-16). We have to ask ourselves how we can bring hope to the people. In the light of the praxis of Jesus we cannot push that hope entirely to an eschatological level, something that happens "when we die". Christianity is not an alternative to this world; it is a guide to live well in this world so that this world itself can be transformed into the pre-figuration of the world to come. We have to insist on the salvific character of history and life in history. Our involvement in history must make God's presence effective. It is a question of the relation between salvation and liberation.

Mission today must change the perspective from the past crusade against other religions, including the aggressive proclamation with claims of exclusivism, to an effective solidarity with the suffering. It is a participation in the brokenness of people, in their hopes, disappointments, and anxieties. Instead of an imposing and dominating attitude the Christians should have the spirit of fellow-pilgrims. Since the Christian community inherit a common origin and common destiny with the rest of people (*Nostra Aetate* 1) they are pilgrims along with others. In this pilgrimage of solidarity, Christians become a people manifesting the God-experience in Jesus Christ. This in turn becomes an attraction, an invitation, a sharing in the form of storytelling, leaving the decision to the listener. That is the type of proclamation to which the modern world is ready to listen.

Jesus was interested in people and their problems. He backed up his preaching with deeds of compassion and acceptance; he promoted the Jubilee spirit of equality, sharing, participation and reconciliation. Similarly, we are invited to shift our emphasis from an attitude of uniqueness to the God-experience and the living of the same experience. True, there is a danger that the God-experience can tend to remain on the vertical level and it is precisely here that Christianity can make its contribution:

the true path to God is through one's neighbour. Thus, mission becomes a process of mutual complementarity and harmony as Pope John Paul II has taught.[40]

Religions take pride in themselves and in their cultural values, but they are often open to mutual enrichment in the midst of the plurality of religions. This requires a greater awareness of the dignity of the individual. Modern concentration of people tends to anonymity, leaving little room for the individual. As opposed to mass movements and mega media projects, Christians must remind themselves how Jesus' approach was personal, directed to the individual. Human society at every level and in every place requires this concern for the individual. However, today society is accused of being too individualistic. Perhaps a loving concern for the individual is needed.

Today, like the prophets of the Old Testament, the church must be able to read and interpret the signs of the times from God's viewpoint. This involves conflict and risk insofar as the message may go against the vested interests of the privileged and the powerful, the monopolizers of the riches of the world whose selfishness and callous blindness deprive many of their right to have the basic requirements for leading a life consonant with human dignity.

Prophetic service is two-sided, involving God and God's perspective as well as that of humans and human equality that has been derailed by the greed and selfishness of the powerful. Hence prophetic ministry is different from sheer social reform. Prophets provoke people to return to their true religious commitment where one cannot detach the divine from the human. Jesus' mission was certainly focused on God whom he experienced as the intimate parent (*Abba*), but expressed in terms of his concern for the neighbour. It was a proclamation of the nature of humanity, derived from the nature of God. In other words, human beings and their life context is the field in which the church has to exercise and manifest its mission. As Gustavo Guttierrez has pointed out, mission is not only a question of geographic space but a matter of human space as well. The "human landscape" is the true locale of mission. [41]

God is not a monster whose sole concern is self-glory, but the one who is honoured when a neighbour is accepted and respected. This is the greatest need today. One may say that we do not need new religions as living the existing religions according to the will of God, leading to the divine reign, the divine "Household", God's future. The Christian role is not that of denying the validity of other religions, but of affirming the humanity of human beings. A Christian must be engaged with humanity and all that is related to it, because the God whom the Christian has experienced in Jesus Christ follows the same path. There is no Christian service divorced from human life in history.

The Christian preoccupation should not be over the 'right' religion that leads to God, but the right channels through which God reaches humans today. The latter becomes the test of the former. In the midst of injustices and oppression condemning millions to a dehumanized existence, God, as we have experienced in Jesus Christ, is not thinking of the embellishments of the liturgy or the niceties of the doctrinal formulations, but the elimination of the inhuman conditions in which the poor are embedded. Theology must express itself in a "humanology" grappling with the human problems that we face today, equally, the gentle treatment of the environment and animals to alleviate suffering.

Most scripture scholars would emphasize the apocalyptic character of the kingdom movement where the socially, politically and economically marginalized people experience the divine vindication. Following Jesus is not primarily a matter of believing Jesus' words, rather it is a matter of accepting Jesus' lifestyle, following his program of ushering in the divine reign for the poor of our times, here and now. Albert Schweitzer, scripture scholar, realizing the true spirit of the mission of Jesus gave up a teaching career in Europe and preaching religion, to become a medical doctor and serve the people of Africa, at the age of thirty. For Schweitzer was convinced eschatology in Jesus is apocalypses, that is the end time in God's manifestation today, here and now.[42] A similar picture emerges from the vision of Jan Jaworski, chief surgeon, Kundiawa Hospital, PNG, qualified in general surgery, orthopaedics and traumatology, vascular surgery and other medical fields, becoming a Catholic priest at the age of forty four to bring the blessings of the Kingdom to the people of PNG combining priesthood and the medical profession.[43]

When we are confronted with the spectre of starvation deaths, violence, the commoditization of human persons, international conflicts not infrequently ignited by the powerful nations of the world, global warming triggered by human consumerism, the diverting of food crops for the production of bio fuels and the spread of HIV/AIDS, we are reminded of God's concern: "I have seen their affliction, I have heard their cry. ... I am sending you to lead my people out of Egypt" (Ex 3:7-10).

Struggling for the creation of a new humanity in the midst of suffering and dehumanizing forces is a key aspect of mission today. It is a struggle to win historical selfhood and subject-hood for the non-people of our times. The emerging new humanity can only be understood in the context of alienation, exploitation and marginalization. This makes the search for community inseparable from the search for new humanity. In the existing situation of the poor crushed by fears, fear of not having anything to eat, fear of eviction, fear of extortion and fear of violence, we cannot be in a genuine community. In the eyes of the powerful, the poor are the problem people. This is a gross mis-designation. The mis-described and the dehumanized must be restored to their right to name the reality they experience. Naming the reality is the biblical symbol of empowerment (Gen 2:19-20).

Concluding Remarks

This write up is basically an attempt to integrate and apply Christian ministry in the light of the Bible and the teachings of the Catholic church, challenging any dualism that bedevils normal Christian thinking, limiting God's transforming work to spiritual realities and assigning earthly matters to secular specialists. A truly wholistic approach to Christian ministry rooted in biblical truth is essential to church's mission today. The God of justice and righteousness for all the earth, a God who stood on the side of the oppressed and exploited, and opposed every form of systemic evil, is the God whom we encounter in the Bible. The same perspective is continued in the Kingdom ministry of Jesus which was a distancing from any form of injustice and discrimination. People could experience what it might mean to be if God were ruling. In this perspective, engagement in development is proclaiming the gospel always, not in word but in deed. This aspect of the Christian mission is reflected in the teachings of the Catholic magisterium which can be summarised as: Between mission and development/liberation there are three-fold links: anthropological, theological and evangelical. It is making the gospel a good news to the people.

Endnotes

[1] Frederick Herzog, *God-Walk: Liberation Shaping Dogmatics*, Maryknoll, N.Y.: Orbis Books, 1988, 46.

[2] I am influenced by Bryant L. Myers for the phrase transformational development. Bryant L. Myers, *Walking with the Poor: Principles and Practices of Transformational Development*, Maryknoll, N.Y.: Orbis Books, 1999.

[3] Michael P. Todaro & Stephen C. Smith, *Economic Development*, London: Addison-Wesley, 2009, 12.

[4] In September 2000 the UN adopted 8 Millennium Development goals to be achieved by 2015: eradicate poverty and hunger, universal primary education, equality of gender and empowerment of women, reduce child mortality, improved maternal health, combat HIV/AIDS, malaria and other diseases, sustainable environment and global partnership. (Todaro & Smith, *Economic Development*, 24).

[5] Judith A. Merkle, *From the Heart of the Church: The Catholic Social Tradition*, Collegeville, Minnesota: Liturgical Press, 2004, 113.

[6] Dominic Crossan, *The Birth of Christianity: Discovering What Happened in the Years Immediately after the Execution of Jesus*, New York: Harper One, 1999, 182.

[7] Jeffrey A. Fager, Land Tenure and the Biblical Jubilee, JSOT Series 155, Sheffield, 1987, 27, in Dominic Crossan, *The Birth of Christianity*, 182.

[8] Crossan, *The Birth of Christianity*, 208.

[9] N.T. Wright, *Jesus and the Victory of God*, Minneapolis: Fortress Press, 1996, xvii.

[10] N.T. Wright, "The Mission and Message of Jesus," in Marcus J. Borg & N.T. Wright, *The Meaning of Jesus*, San Francisco: Harper, 1999, 35.

[11] Crossan, *The Birth of Christianity*, 325.

[12] Warren Carter, *Matthew and the Margins: A Socio-political and Religious Reading* (New York: Orbis Books, 2000).

[13] Carter, *Matthew and the Margins*, 136-139.

[14] G.S.Key, "The Table Fellowship of Jesus: Its Significance for Dalit Christians in India Today," *Jeevadhara* XIII/74(1983):85.

[15] Dominic Crossan, *Jesus: A Revolutionary Biography* (San Francisco: Harper, 1994), 71.

[16] Joachim Jeremias, *New Testament Theology: The Proclamation of Jesus* (London: SCM, 1971), 115-116.

[17] Donal Dorr, "Christian Mission and the Millennium Development Goals," *Sedos Bulletin* 39-1/2(2007): 24.

[18] Daniel Groody, *Globalization, Spirituality and Justice* (New York: Orbis Books, 2007), 49.

[19] T.Megilla, 4.11, in Richard Burridge, *Imitating Jesus: An Inclusive approach to New Testament Ethics* (Grand Rapids: Eerdmans, 2007), 122.

[20] Joachim Gnilka, *Jesus of Nazareth: Message and History* (Massachusetts: Hendrickson, 1997), 64.

[21] N.T.Wright, *Jesus and the Victory of God,* 203.

[22] N.T. Wright, *The Challenge of Jesus: Rediscovering Who Jesus Was and Is* (Downers Grove: Intervarsity Press, 1999), 38.

[23] Diarmuid O'Murchu, *Catching up with Jesus: A Gospel Story for our Time* (New York: Crossroad, 2005), 5.

[24] Bruce M Metzger (ed.), *New Revised Standard Version Exhaustive Concordance* (Nashville: Thomas Nelson, 1991), 1040-41.

[25] N.T. Wright, *Jesus and the Victory of God,* 477. E.P.Sanders, *The Historical Figure of Jesus* (London: Penguin Books, 1993), 80.

[26] N.T. Wright, *Jesus and the Victory of God,* 483.

[27] John Meier, *The Aims of Jesus* (London: SCM, 1979), 199.

[28] Neil Ormerod, *Creation, Grace, and Redemption* (New York: Orbis Books, 2007), 90.

[29] Dominic Crossan and Jonathan L. Reed, *In Search of Paul. How Jesus's Apostle Opposed Rome's Empire with God's Kingdom: A New Vision of Paul's Words and World* (New York: Harper Collins, 2004), 381.

[30] Corssan and Reed, *In Search of Paul, 382.*

[31] N.T. Wright, *Jesus and the Victory of god, 273.*

[32] Tertullian, *Disciplinary, Moral and Ascetical Works,* (ed.) Hermigild Dressler, *Fathers of the Church* Vol 40 (Washington: University of America Press, 1977), 299-300.

[33] Ormerod, *Creation, Grace, and Redemption,* 94-95.

[34] N.T. Wright, *Jesus and the Victory of God, 105.*

[35] Judith A. Merkle, *From the Heart of the Church,* 93.

[36] Judith A. Merkle, *From the Heart of the Church,* 12.

[37] Roger Haight, *Jesus Symbol of God* (New York: Orbis Books, 1999), 106-107.

[38] Roger Haight, *Jesus Symbol of God, 26.*

[39] Antony Raj, "Disobedience: A Legitimate Act for Dalit Liberation," in Arvind Nirmal (ed.), *Towards a Common Dalit Theology* (Delhi: ISPCK, 1988,) 51.

[40] John Paul II, *Ecclesia in Asia* (Vatican: Libreria Editrice Vaticana, 1999), n 6, p.15.

[41] Gustavo Guttierrez, "Mission et I'signes des Temps," *Spiritus* 41 (2000): 184.

[42] Albert Schweitzer, *On the Edge of the Primeval Forest* (London: Collins Fontana Books, 1970).

[43] Jo Chandler, "The man with magic hands," *The Age: Insight*, Saturday September 18, (2010): 10.

Chapter - 4

Margins and the
Mission of Advocacy

In our globalized world with its struggle for dignity and justice advocacy has become an ardent form of mission. This is all the more significant in a post-Christendom and post-colonial world where the Church has found itself displaced from the power equations. A major portion of the Bible is a narrative of advocacy, whether of God for the marginalized Israelites in bondage in Egypt, or of Abraham for the people of Sodom and Gomorrah or of the prophets for the poor and the exploited. Jesus' own mission, largely, was of the nature of advocacy for the poor. In this spirit the chapter argues how a major expression of the contemporary mission of the church is advocacy for the margins making the church a hope-inducing sign.

The idea of advocacy has become all too familiar in the secular society making it an essential feature of modern polity. Yet in missiological literature, by and large, it has remained a rare theme. This is all the more significant since advocacy is a key ingredient of the bible and it could bring a freshness of perspective to mission theory and practice.

One of the challenging ideas of the Bible, as Jonathan Sacks, author and Rabbi, has pointed out, is the ethics of responsibility, i.e., God invites humans to be partners in the work of creation – naming, tilling, caring for the earth, building the ark and so on.[1] For long the Christian community considered its partnership with God as a call to bring an otherworldly salvation to the miserable inhabitants of the colonial world. The trade-inspired exploratory expeditions of Christopher Columbus ignited the missionary vision of European religious congregations to save the souls of the poor heathens, the vintage "being gathered by the devil and the flesh," depriving Christ "of enjoying the possession of the souls which he purchased with his blood."[2]

Thankfully, the conquest, expansion and displacement model of mission has rapidly declined without much regret. This is a challenge to return to the original biblical spirit. As John Corrie has argued, the eclipse of the past "managerial missiology," "with its aggressive approach, its targets and goals, its well-oiled financial and resourceful structures, and its well-developed sending strategies, must enable the church to opt in favour of an incarnational, relational, culturally diverse, flexible and spontaneous model of doing mission."[3] We need to retrieve the mission of the Lord who was anointed "to proclaim the good news to the poor" (Lk 4: 18). A major consequence of the modern globalization process and people movement, for whatever reasons, is that a sizable number of people are pushed to the periphery of nations and societies. This has prompted Pope Francis to emphasize "a constant outreach to the peripheries" as an important aspect of mission today.[4]

This paper argues how advocacy is a significant form of the proclamation of the good news to the poor in the post-colonial world, paving the way for ushering in the acceptable year of the Lord.

Biblical Foundation

As Christopher Wright has rightly emphasized the Bible is more than just advocacy, but the advocacy dimension cannot be underestimated.[5] Even a casual reader cannot fail to be impressed by the centrality of advocacy in the Bible. No doubt, the Bible is a narration of God's reaching out to humans and creation. However, this reaching out is woven into the power and pattern of advocacy.

Obviously, the biblical vision of our life with God is God's reign, the Kingdom, that manifests itself in a socio-religious and political transformation. In this the Bible "combines sharp political criticism and passionate political advocacy," writes Marcus Borg.[6] We have in the Bible not only the passionate protesting of injustice, but equally a passionate advocacy for justice as well, based on a God of love, justice and compassion. Borg calls this biblical option for the margins "a political passion,"[7] for it is the result of the "systemic injustice, sources of unnecessary human misery, created by unjust political, economic and social systems."[8]

The biblical concern for the margins is concretely expressed in its innovative commands: Yearly tithes were to be gathered for the poor, and farmers were to leave some of their crops behind for widows and aliens to glean (Lev 19:9-10); loans to the needy were without interest, and if they could not repay in seven years, they were to be forgiven (Dt 15:1-3); if hard times forced a farmer to sell his land, it was to be returned in the year of jubilee (Lev 25:28).

Lois Tverberg shows how the distinctive feature of the Torah was its great concern for society's vulnerable.[9] Israel's very first experience of Yahweh occurs in the context of advocacy. Yahweh has seen their affliction and heard their cry and has come to plead for them through Moses (Ex 3:9-10). Moses who encountered the divine at the burning bush does not come off with deepened convictions about the physical nature of God, but with the attitudinal, psychological nature of the God who is moved by the affliction of the slaves in Egypt. It is shaped by the divine passion for the poor, the divine undertaking of "a justice marked by enough bread and freedom from debt, worry, and sorrow."[10]

Redemption, in the Bible, is not primarily an otherworldly or an after-death reality, but most of the time it deals with life on earth as we can see from the Exodus. Exodus-shaped redemption demands exodus-shaped mission. It is a holistic understanding of God's mission. This is significant when we speak of advocacy as a major expression of mission today.

Most of the biblical prophets are moving in this spirit. They perceive how the existing reality is not in conformity with the divine plan. The powerful make use of their power and influence to exploit the poor and the Prophets protest against it and plead for the cause of the poor.[11]

When we come to the gospels, we see how Jesus, "the decisive revelation of God,"[12] without denying whatever he is believed to be, was a social prophet in the line of the Old Testament prophets. The mission of Jesus Christ is to be situated in the context of the Jewish messianic expectations. There is no uniform expectation of the Messiah in the Jewish tradition,[13] though it began with the hope of a restoration of the Davidic kingship, a new king from the house of David who would unite the kingdom of Israel and Judah. The Messiah is the one promised and anointed by God to deliver the Jewish people from oppression and to bring in a new era on earth.[14] From this emerges the hope of a Saviour King who would appear at the end of time to usher in a new era.[15]

Jesus began his ministry, particularly in the Marcan gospel, with the claim that the hoped for Messiah has come.[16] Marcus Borg writes: "Mark affirms at the beginning of his gospel that Jesus is *the* Messiah, the hoped-for and longed-for anointed one of Israel. The good news is the story of Jesus the Messiah."[17] The Marcan inaugural proclamation, "The time is fulfilled, and the kingdom of God is at hand" (1:15), indicates not only the beginning of Jesus' public activity, but names its content as well.[18]

Jesus' option for the socially and religiously marginalized is obvious in all the four gospels. He was the prophet of the Kingdom. He was inclusive of all who were left on the margins, economically, socially, religiously or according to gender. In his inaugural teaching at Nazareth, according to Luke, Jesus selects Isaiah 61:1-2 showing how he has been sent to preach the good news to the poor, all those who are on the periphery – the blind, the lame, the leprosy-affected – all those who are bound in any way. The divine goodness reaches them as an experience of the good news that the long-awaited messiah sets in. It is a manifestation that, "God accepts them and, although they are empty-handed, Jesus himself rejoices with them", observes Lucien Richard.[19]

The most visible public activity that demonstrated this prophetic advocacy was his all-inclusive meal practice.[20] As Marcus Borg insists, the salvation that Jesus proclaimed was seldom about an afterlife, "rather, it is about transformation this side of death."[21]

Similarly, Geza Vermes, in the context of speaking about the religion of Jesus writes: "In the religion of Jesus, customary priorities were reversed. Not only did he embrace prophetic preferences, placing the poor, the orphans, the widows and the prisoners before the conventionally devout, but he offered privileged treatment to the sick and to the pariahs of society."[22]

The prayer that Jesus taught, with its Kingdom petitions, is advocacy *par excellence*! It is not only a prayer of Jesus' vision, but equally an invitation to us to participate in God's vision. For John Dominic Crossan it is the Lord's "revolutionary manifesto", proclaiming "the radical vision of justice that is the core of Israel's biblical tradition."[23] Jesus' message is not about believing a set of doctrines about him, rather it is about the coming of God's reign, with its challenge to engage oneself in the same mission. We need not only have faith in Jesus but also develop the faith of Jesus. As Ray Vander Loan has pointed out, "To be a disciple of Jesus I need to know why and how he lived out his faith, so that I could follow him more closely."[24]

Though God's Word Incarnate, the greatest success of Jesus was his reading the signs of the times, i.e., the Jewish society with its religion stood in need of a transformation from its legalism and ritualism, and priestly careerism. He began with the baptism of John when he experienced the divine grip on him. From then on there is no turning back. Robert Funk invites our attention to the fact how some of the earliest collections of Jesus' sayings and deeds, the Q and the gospel of Thomas, do not contain the passion narrative. More important was his ministry of the Kingdom, which they expected to be completed by the second coming soon to happen.[25]

This dialogue of the gospel with the contemporary times must lead to an involvement of advocacy for the world. The miracles of Jesus were not for proving his divinity, but to show how God is already taking steps to transform the society. Today advocacy can release the organic energy of the gospel for the transformation of the world. Advocacy for the restoration of the divine plan for humankind must fire church's evangelistic imagination.

Evangelism and Advocacy

The primary service of the church today is to bring the messianic hope to the world of today especially for those suffering various forms of slavery rooted in the structures of power and domination. Poverty with all its ingredients constitutes a basic cause of misery and marginalization in God's creation where all have a place with harmonious relationship with one another.

Yet this is disrupted through human selfishness tending to power and possession engendering inequality and dehumanization. In his address to the United Nations' Food and Agriculture Office in 1998, Pope John Paul II invited the participating nations to work for solutions which would lead to a world "in which there are no longer people living side-by-side in hunger and others in opulence, people who are extremely poor and those who are extremely wealthy, people who lack the bare necessities and others who waste things without thinking twice. Humanity cannot tolerate such contrasts between poverty and wealth."[26]

Unfortunately, this is a scandal our world tolerates with ease and admits in a matter-of-fact spirit. This is an area in which the Church has to spend itself to bring the awareness of the gravity of the fact and the injustice involved to all people, challenging them to be converted so that the divine reign can come for the poor of the world. As Roger Etchegaray has emphasized, "The scandal is that today we can repeat and repeat, in analysis after analysis that extreme poverty still exists when we have the means to eliminate it. The scandal is that we can enthuse about the progress of globalization while this primeval form of the failure of true human cohabitation continues to exist, and in some, areas to grow."[27]

It is taken for granted that the global society is going through great change, though the magnitude of change and the response required may not be that clear. What is even less known is the changes that began with Adam Smith's economic theory of the maximum amount of wealth production when one acts upon selfish interest rather than listening to any divine promptings, adding that an invisible hand would ensure the trickling down of the wealth to the poor as well. This in turn triggered off the western industrial revolution and economic growth along with the trickling down of the wealth to the poorer sections of the society, as Adam Smith had visualized. However, the sad part of the whole development was that European powers launched into the "new world" of Asia, Africa and Latin America to produce a maximum amount of wealth for themselves without any sanction to ensure that part of that wealth trickled down to the poor of these nations. To a large extent the woes of the so called third world today are related to this surge of the industrial revolution.[28]

This, arguably, has serious missionary implication in so far as mission to the south was under the shadow of colonialism. The spirit of the times can be gauged from the infamous justification of the colonial and missionary enterprise by Sir Francis Drake: "Their gain shall be in the knowledge of our Faith, and ours such riches as their country hath."[29]

This realization must impel the churches in the west to exercise a new form of mission, not for the expansion of home churches, but through international advocacy for the poor of these former colonies so that people bound to their economic woes and dehumanized life by forces outside their control can experience the blessings of the arrival of the divine reign. As Pope Francis observed while receiving the secretary general of the United Nations, Ban Ki-moon, we need to promote "a true, worldwide ethical mobilization that will spread and put into practice a shared ideal of fraternity and solidarity, especially with regard to the poorest and those most excluded."[30]

Down through the centuries the church has exercised a major role in social and political change not only through its many educational and social institutions but also through its advocacy as in the renowned instance of Bartolomeo de Las Casas. A classic example is the role played by Pope John Paul II to usher in democracy in East Europe.

In contemporary times the role played by what is known as liberation theology and the articulate theologians such as Leonardo Boff, Gustavo Gutierrez, Jon Sobrino and others for social transformation and political action in the context of injustice, more so in Latin America, cannot be ignored. Political advocacy has been an area at the service of the powerless and voiceless that the church has engaged itself into influence the decision makers to adopt policies that are beneficial to the poor and marginalized. Though the church is not and cannot be a political institution, as the sacrament of the divine reign, its political role, the political content of its service, cannot be ignored. It not only reflects on the social implications of the gospel but somehow makes it operational at the service of the disenfranchised. Most of the martyrdoms in modern times, like that of Archbishop Romero, and many in other places like India, are, in fact the result of this political advocacy.[31]

Racism and Advocacy

Xenophobia and ethnocentrism existed from ancient times, but the age of enlightenment became a watershed moment in the development of modern racism.[32] Pierre van den Berghe describes racism as "any set of beliefs that organic, genetically transmitted differences, whether real or imagined, between human groups are intrinsically associated with the presence or absence of certain socially relevant abilities or characteristics, hence that such differences are a legitimate basis of invidious distinctions between groups socially defined as races."[33]

Racism does not believe in the individual but in membership in a particular human group, attributing all characteristics to the group's physical heritage. "In the racist world-view there is no human individuality. Each individual is merely an inevitable manifestation of the collective to which s/he belongs, with the nature of that collective determined by shared heredity."[34]

This vision needs to be challenged and the church has to advocate a value system that believes in the common origin and shared nature of all human beings, showing how race is socially constructed. Advocacy against Apartheid is a success story against any form of racial oppression. The church will always argue against any claim of racial supremacism justifying the right of one race to rule or exploit another race, or not allowing the space for another. The church will have to be sensitive also as not to promote racism even in theology by foisting theology from any one particular geographical area as universal theology while describing theologies that have developed at the periphery as local theologies!

An Alternative Future

Jacques Matthey, commenting on 1 Corinthians 1 where the apostle Paul reminds his readers of God's purpose of electing people from the down trodden of the world so as to shame the powerful and wise, and on James 2:5 pointing to God's calling the poor as a challenge to the rich, and the church's duty not to make distinctions, writes how both the authors in different ways remind us to have a spirituality of taking God's priorities seriously, "both for life within as well as without the churches, and let itself be shaped by a bias for the poor, marginalized, despised, suffering, vulnerable, and powerless."[35]

We want a world without division and exclusion, which is our alternative vision, based on the Bible. The voice of this vision is advocacy, in contrast to the politically expedient solution of expanding production. It is a time when violence becomes rare, women can feel fully integrated in the society, and children are not exploited. Opposition to Violence, in particular, is an area that is to be accentuated. The first impulse of religious thought ought to be that of peace. Yet, it is no secret that most religions have been instruments of violence even as religious scriptures, including the Bible, cannot disclaim elements of violence.

No wonder then, "many people connect violence with religion generally," as Jan van Henten wrote.[36] The attack on the New York twin towers in 2001, triggering a new round of violence, is a typical example of the link between religion and violence. Yet, religions in general and Christianity in particular have to become a healing power where violence holds sway through advocacy for peace, though always mindful of justice as well.

Pope Francis' inclusion of a Rabbi and a Muslim leader in his team during his visit to Jordan, West Bank and Israel for the May 24-26, 2014 trip is a sign of the key role of advocacy for peace. In fact, some commentators have compared the image of the church, after the initiative of the Pope, to a "field hospital" to bring healing to battle-scared warriors.[37]

Domestic violence against women is a universal issue that has to figure in Christian discourse on advocacy. Even in Australia most divorces are attributed to domestic violence. Gender discrimination in any form is violence and women anywhere in the world are victims of it in many forms including the exclusion from religious ministries and decision making.

Kingdom-centred ministry

Society in general, in most spheres of life like religion, politics, culture, economics and others, is structured in such a way that the powerful are at the centre with the powerless at the periphery. This has to be altered so that all can feel at home, participating in the resources as well as decision making. This is very much associated with justice and human rights and in this context the United Nations' Declaration of Human Rights 1948 assumes great significance. Dehumanizing marginalization with little share in the fruits of their creativity is the lot of a vast majority of people.

It is a matter of encouragement that the Catholic Church since Pope Leo XIII's encyclical *Rerum Novarum* (New Order of Things) has been a strong advocate of the working class and social justice in general. A series of encyclicals and church documents have contributed to the amelioration of life for the workers in general. Similarly, the WCC Affirmation on Mission and Evangelism (Busan, Korea, 2013) called for a mission from the margins. "Through struggles in and for life, marginalized people are reservoirs of the active hope, collective resistance, and perseverance that are needed to remain faithful to the promised reign of God."[38]

Advocacy, in the context of the Kingdom, simply is a "strategy to generate social change,"[39] more so in the context of the existing world situation of marginalization and injustice. This requires a sound acquaintance with the ground reality with its associated problems and forces that control the reality. This is an area for the church to get deeper understanding even as it did in the past with regard to cultures and religions. The church has to familiarize itself with the systems, structures and social forces that shape the society, the pull and push factors, population, freedom of religion, social development, national product, state of life expectancy, environmental change and, in general, all those factors related to holistic development.

The church aligns with the margins allowing the margins to speak and not only for themselves. In this the church is aware also of the biblical polarity, relation between the particular and the universal, the few for the many. Abraham's call to become a blessing for the nations (Gen 12:1-3) is manifestative of God's economy of the few serving the many. As Ross Blackburn reminds us: "The tension between the universality of the goal (all nations) and the particularity of the means (through you) is right there from the very beginning of Israel's journey through the pages of the Old Testament."[40] However, we have to remind ourselves, "committing oneself to justice, peace and ecological integrity demands prophetic living, prophetic speech and prophetic action individually, communally and institutionally."[41]

What we are interested in is not so much levelling economic inequalities, but in ensuring economic security for all. The response to rising economic inequality is not cutting wealth at the top, but empowering the poor so that they can get richer and poverty is eliminated, by providing decent opportunities and security for all, for as Franklin Delano Roosevelt argued:

"A clear realization of the fact that true individual freedom cannot exist without economic security and independence."[42] It includes a right to a good education, a useful and remunerative job, a right to earn enough to provide food, clothing, shelter and medical care for one's family and freedom from economic fears of old age, sickness, accident and unemployment.

Concluding Remarks

Similar to the past evangelical method of education for developing good leaders and enlightened population, today we have to move to social analysis to point out the ills of the society, with a view to foster a better vision of society, providing models of social change to ensure a genuinely inclusive society, especially of the poor and the excluded ones.

In the context of the growing significance of the impact of advocacy, as manifested through the working of the United Nations and the many NGOs churches are to ready themselves to be engaged in this form of missioning as well as make adequate resources for this ministry. Generating social transformation through diverse ways is acknowledged as an effective way of following the Lord, who "went about doing good" (Act 10:38). Influencing the leaders of nations to carry the society along with a sense of purpose and mission is a service the importance of which cannot be exaggerated. Taming the dominant sections of a society so that remedial steps are taken to empower the powerless and the disenfranchised so that they can also sit along with the powerful and the privileged and thus build an inclusive society is a major paradigm of mission today.

Such a mission makes the church a sign of hope for the contemporary world, especially for those who are on the margins of this world. It brings a freshness of perspective, i.e., the church is a community that is in solidarity with the suffering and the downtrodden peoples, more so due to the denial of justice and equality. This resounded in Archbishop Romero of El Salvador's advocacy for the margins when he addressed the soldiers on March 23, 1980, the day before his assassination: "We are your people. The peasants you kill are your own brothers and sisters. When you hear the voice of the man commanding you to kill, remember instead the voice of God. Thou shall not kill. In the name of God, in the name of the tormented people whose cries rise up to heaven, I beseech you, I beg you, I command you, stop the repression."[43]

Endnotes

[1] Jonanathan Sacks, *To Heal a Fractured World: The Ethics of Responsibility* (London: Continuum, 2005), 17.

[2] Letter of Franciscan General, Francisco de los Angeles 1523. See McKennie, Goodpasture, *Cross and Sword: An Eye Witness History of Christianity in Latin America* (New York: Orbis Books, 1989), 20.

[3] John Corrie, "Migration as a Theologizing Experience: The Promise of Interculturality for Transformative Mission," *Mission Studies* 31(2014): 11.

[4] FRANCIS, "Message of Pope Francis for World Mission Day 2014," www.http//Curia Vatican org. messages. accessed on 29/06/2014.

[5] Christopher Wright, *The Mission of God: Unlocking the Bible's Grand Narrative* (Nottingham: IVP, 2008), 42.

[6] Marcus Borg, *The Heart of Christianity* (New York: Harper, 2003), 126.

[7] *The Heart of Christianity,* 129.

[8] *The Heart of Christianity, 129.*

[9] Lois Tverberg, *Walking in the Dust of Rabbi Jesus* (Grand Rapids: Zondervan 2012), 79.

[10] BORG, *The Heart of Christianity,* 143.

[11] Isaiah 58:6-7; 61:1-2; Jeremiah 9:24; 22:13-14; Amos 4:1; 8:4-6; Micah 6:8, and others

[12] Marcus Borg, *Meeting Jesus in Mark* (London: SPCK, 2011), 3.

[13] Peter Schaefer, *The Jewish Jesus. How Judaism and Christianity Shaped Each other* (Oxford: Princeton University Press, 2012), 223.

[14] Marcus Borg, *Speaking Christian: Recovering the lost meaning of Christian Words* (London: SPCK, 2011), 94.

[15] Schaefer, *The Jewish Jesus,* 223.

[16] Tverberg, *Walking in the Dust of Rabbi Jesus,* 27. Tverberg points out how for Jesus' audience, "to proclaim the Kingdom of God was to make a shocking announcement that God's promised Messiah had arrived, because the task of the Messiah was to establish God's kingdom on earth."

[17] Marcus Borg, *Meeting Jesus in Mark* (London: SPCK, 2011), 20.

[18] Borg, *Meeting Jesus in Mark,* 27.

[19] Lucian Richard, *Christ the Self-Emptying of God* (New York: St Paul, 1997), 31.

[20] Marcus Borg, *The Heart of Christianity,* 91.

[21] Marcus Borg, *Speaking Christian,* 14

[22] Geza Vermes, *Christian Beginnings: From Nazareth to Nicea AD30-325* (London: Penguin Books, 2012), 55-56.

[23] Dominic J. Crossan, *The Greatest Prayer: Rediscovering the Revolutionary Message of the lord's prayer* (New York: Harper One, 2010), 2.

[24] Vermes Ray Vander, "Foreword," *Walking in the Dust of Rabbi Jesus* (Lois Tverberg, Zondervan: Grand Rapids, 2012), 9.

[25] Robert W Funk, *Honest to Jesus* (Rydalmere, NSW: Hodder & Stoughton, 1996), 38-40.

[26] John Paul II, "Address to FAO," quoted in "A Jubilee on Poverty," Cardinal Roger Etchegary, *Sedos Bulletin* 30/3(1998): 67.

[27] Roger Etchegary, "A Jubilee on Poverty," *Sedos Bulletin* 30/3, (1998): 67.

[28] David Smith, *Mission After Christendom* (London: Darton. Longman+Todd, 2003), 23-24.

[29] See David Smith, *Mission After Christendom,* 23.

[30] UCAN India.in/news/Pope-francis-urges-global-redistribution of wealth/24878/daily, accessed on 13.05.2014

[31] Jacob Kavunkal, "Fresh Perspectives in Mission," in *Theological Explorations: Centenary Festschrift in honour of centenarian Josef Neuner,* Jacob Kavunkal (ed) (Delhi: ISPCK, 2008), 103.

[32] Manfred Berg, and Simon Wendt, (eds), *Racism in the Modern World* (New York: Berghahn, 2011), 5.

[33] Pierre van den Bserghe, *Race and Racism, A Comparative Perspective* (New York, 1978), 9, quoted in *Racism in the Modern World,* Manfred Berg, 4.

[34] Berg, and Wendt, *Racism in the Modern World,* 44.

[35] Jacqes Matthey, "Missional Spirituality in the Contemporary World," in *Walk Humbly with the Lord: Church and Mission,* Vigo Mortensen and Andreas Osterlund (eds) (Grand Rapids: Eerdmans, 2010), 256.

[36] Jan van Henten Willem, "Religion, Bible and Violence," in *Coping with Violence in the New Testament*, Pieter Villiers G.R.de and Jan Willem van Henten (eds) (Leiden-Boston: Brill, 2012), 4

[37] Kelly, Michael "The Substance behind Pope Francis' Style," Ucanews. com/news/the-substance-behind-pope-francis-style/70956 (accessed on 20-05-2014).

[38] Jooseop Keum, (ed), *Together Towards Life: Mission and Evangelism in Changing Landscapes* (Geneva: WCC Publications, 2013), 15-16.

[39] Brigid Reynolds and Sean Healy, "Transformation of Society and the Role of Advocacy: An Irish Case Study," *Sedos Bulletin* 31/1(1999): 15.

[40] W. Ross Blackburn, *The God Who Makes Himself Known: The Missionary Heart of the Book of Exodus* (Downers Grove, Illinois: Inter University Press, 2012), 222.

[41] Stephen Bevans and, Roger Schroeder, *Constants in Context: A Theology of Mission for Today* (Maryknoll, N.Y.: Orbis Books, 2004), 377.

[42] See Cass SUNSTEIN, "What is so Wrong with Economic Inequality?" *The Age*, 13 May 2014, p20

[43] Jon Sobrino, *Archbishop Romero: Memories and Reflections* (Maryknoll, N.Y.: Orbis Books, 1990), 116.

Chapter - 5

Migration, Mission and Identity

Migration has become a global phenomenon, involving millions of people, making it a structural reality of contemporary culture. Migration is a complex phenomenon in so far as it can mean people moving from one location to another, either within one's own country or to another, voluntarily or forced by any compulsion of freedom, economy, persecution, natural disaster and others.

It brings many challenges especially that of the identity both of the immigrants as well as that of the host countries. Divine self-reaching out, divine hospitality, is foundational to mission to the migrants. The chapter argues how Christian reaching out to the migrants in acceptance and respect is a need of the hour and this can lead to a multicultural community in the church and in society at large, imparting not only hope to migrants but also for all an identity with alterity.

With its many inbuilt characteristics, migration has become a major context of mission as well. Mission basically is the project towards the continuation of the kingdom of God, inaugurated by Jesus Christ, a new world order characterized by right relationships of justice, concern and compassion. Migration, with its multidimensional demands, has become a serious challenge for the very being of the church as the sacrament of divine hospitality. The church's call to be missionary impels it to reach out to the migrants in justice and compassion offering hope in their struggle for acceptance and identity in a world where dominant groups tend to make the other illegal or outcaste. The biblical mandate to offer hospitality to strangers is built on the fact that all are recipients of the divine hospitality (Dt. 10:19; Lev 19:4; Mt 25:35).

Migration a Global Reality

Migration and the resulting new/transformed identity are well known phenomena of history. The whole biblical narrative is weaved in the context of migration. The bible speaks of the migration of Terah's family, probably a Semitic one, from Ur to Canaan through Haran. The story continues through Abraham's migration to Egypt, the Exodus, Exile, the migration of Jesus' family to Egypt and so on. One may say biblical revelation occurs in the context of migration. It is the story of God who accompanies a migrant people.

The evolution of Indian Identity resulting from the migration of the Aryan speaking people from central Asia to the Indian subcontinent is common knowledge. Later in history we have instances of migration and new identity in the case of the nations of the Americas or Oceania, though in this case it was mixed also with violence, dispossession and disempowerment. Migration was not always inter-continental as there have also been instances of migration to the neighbourhood or bordering states, leading to a new identity such as Northern Ireland or Tripura, in India.

Migration has been a reality ever since one human tribe found the existence of other tribes. What is new is that it has become a key issue of the present history and a global phenomenon since most countries of the globe are either countries of origin of the migrants, or destination or transition countries, or all at the same time. The impact of globalization, facilitated by improved technology of communication and transportation has accelerated the rate of migration. The link between globalization, migration and identity is not only an international reality but it affects even nations as proved by the experience of *Dalit* communities in India that were impacted by globalization prompting a change in identity and, in some cases, there were migrations to elsewhere to escape from the former hostile environment.[1]

Migration has become a very complex phenomenon, not only due to its volume but also due to its types and motivating factors. Not only do we have migrant workers, but we come across also migrants as trainees, students, intra-company transferees, service providers, traders and many others. Some speak of the feminization of migration due to the increasing number of women who are moving out,[2] in contrast to the traditional migration of women associated with male migration or family migration.

Though the exact figures are difficult to ascertain, the United Nations has tried to estimate the gigantic size of the problem by putting together the information of periodic censuses of the member states and according to the UN agencies in the year 2000 there were 175 million migrants, up from 105 in 1985.[3] In 2010, nearly 250 million people globally were labelled as migrants, forming 3% of the then estimated 7 billion world population.[4]

According to the UN Migration Report of September 2019 there were 272 million international migrants, continuing an upward trend in all world regions and outpacing the growth percentage of world population. Currently, the migrants comprise 3.5 percent of the global population.[5] The type of migration also makes it difficult to assess the level of migration. Frequently there is the come across the issue of illegal/irregular migrants whose number is on the increase due to the tightened immigration policies of the host countries as well as the growing emigration pressures of the countries of origin.

Though in many instances migration involves the free choice of the migrants themselves, it is well-known how often it is dictated by other factors such as economic, political, religious or even cultural, indicating the existing imbalances of these factors on a regional or global level.

Migration is not only from global south to global north, but also from north to north or from south to south. As Katalina Tahaafe-Williams has argued, a major impact of the global migration is the challenge that cultural and ethnic diversity has brought to western churches[6]. The Netherlands constitutes a model case of modern migration and identity issue due to its two-way migration, outward and inward. From 2000 to 2009 an average 107,000 Dutch people migrated to other countries like, Canada, the US and Australia. In the same period the number of immigrants per year to the Netherlands amounted to 128,000, mainly from Spain, Greece, Morocco, Turkey and other countries.[7] Obviously this creates a lasting impact on Dutch cultural identity. Similarly, according to a BBC report, in 2011 42,000 Irish citizens migrated, mainly to Canada, Australia and the United States while even more immigrants have come into Ireland affecting Irish identity.[8]

Space and focus do not allow me to dwell on the manifold challenges faced by migrants. Hence I highlight only some aspects associated with mission. Based on the media reports one is frequently led to the impression that the majority of the migrants are illegal arrivals, if not outright criminals. The prominent aspect of viewing the migrant situation frequently is legality often leading to the link between immigration and security, exclusively centred round the host state, with little concern for the security of the immigrants themselves and they are offered little protection. The host state adopts policies insensitive to humanitarian concerns and blind to the human rights of the persons involved.

Similarly, in so far as each state's duty is primarily, though not exclusively, to its own citizens, and in so far as there is no recognized right to immigrate, foreigners will be admitted to a nation subject to considerations of advantage to the in-taking state. The only contrary principle is the duty not to turn aside those seeking political asylum when founded on genuine fear of persecution.[9]

One of the leading aspects of migration is the question of identity both for the migrants, for the host country and for the countries of origin. For instance, it is estimated that over two out of every five tertiary graduates from Guyana and Jamaica are residing in the US.[10] One frequently hears of the brain drain factor that affects practically all the developing and poor nations, with its obvious developmental consequences leaving an impact also on their identity[11].

As far as the identity is concerned, some of the related issues are: the insistence of the host countries on homogeneity, at the exclusion of the cultural other. Equally, there can be a persistent refusal on the part of the migrants to assimilate the local culture by becoming ethnic enclaves. This, in turn, can lead to a sense of marginalization and feelings of inhospitality. As Lefebvre and Susin show us, "Through migration, ethnic cultures penetrate nations and reconfigure societies with their values, their religions, and their ways of life,"[12] making it imperative to have a new 'catholicity'.

Mission to the Migrants

Mission is moulded by the theology presupposed as mission is the putting into practice of the theological principles that are taken for granted. The Asian bishops observed that "the alarming number of migrants, refugees, returnees and internally displaced persons, and the emerging economic, cultural, religious and moral issues are certainly a pastoral challenge for the church, demanding an adequate and urgent pastoral response. As for the church in Asia, these pose urgent pastoral challenges to incorporate life-giving, service-oriented programs within the pastoral mission of the church. The church should join hands with all who are concerned with the rights of the migrants and their situation, keeping in mind that the migrants themselves are the primary agents of change."[13]

Authors like Lucien Richard[14] and George Newlands and Allen Smith[15] speak of the Hospitality of God, understood as the divine unconditionality. Newlands and Allen Smith have suggested hospitality as key to the universe, as key indeed to the undergirding structure of divine action, quite as significant as the laws of relativity or thermodynamics.[16] Mission is translating divine hospitality into effective service to humanity and creation. Looking through the lens of divine hospitality we need to reframe our understanding of mission from that of God calling or sending us to diffuse Christianity, to plant the church or to save human beings, to a more positive and participative one, participating in the self-expansive movement of God as the expression of the exuberant goodness, to reach out to others. Mission becomes a journey with God, the "pure unbounded hospitality"[17] without any tinge of elimination, assimilation or domination.

It is this perspective of divine self-reaching out, *extensio Dei* that undergirds mission in the context of Migrants. Paulo Suess has emphasized *Missio Dei* reminds us of the biblical injunction, "By their fruit you shall know them" (Mt 7:20) and not by their liturgies or theologies."[18] Then, as Paulo Suess wrote, "[i]t can mean something to people who are wandering around rootless, unwanted and blind, and can speak to them of the love of God,"[19] in our case the migrants.

The root metaphor of mission as divine self-reaching out is the 'other'. The other is an invitation for the Christian to reach out, in so far as the Christian self-realization, and the self-realization of the other, require that both are to be transformed into 'thou' from a mere 'it' category, to use the language of Martin Buber. It is an invitation to relationship and communion bestowing an identity on both partners in this dialogue. The other becomes the grammar of interpreting the scripture and expressing mission. That expression, that practice, is the expression of Christian existence as presented in the judgement scene in the Matthean gospel (25:31-46). The migrant is the other that the church encounters most frequently. Mission to the migrants implies not only the initial help but a true welcome that goes all the way in accompanying migrants in their effort to integration.

The genuine identity of any Christian community is this other-centeredness. In this sense the migrants become the challenge for the Christian community to retrieve its foundational memory, the root metaphor of self-giving. Migrants, frequently victims of hidden and sometimes even overt racism, become the prophetic invitation of the universal sign of God's self-reaching out, self-disclosure in God's Word Incarnate. The excluded migrant becomes the key to experience the local identity of the kenotic Christ who was the localization of the Other, by entering into solidarity with the marginalized and the poor. God's story as unfolded in the Bible and more so in the ministry of God's word incarnate, is a story of giving identity to the marginalized, to the vulnerable, characteristics that we explicitly come across in the story of migrants. Generally speaking, it is a story of victimhood, powerlessness and rejection, a story of the struggle against the powers of this world. They are to be accepted and integrated as partners in the local church, bestowing on them a genuine identity.

Knowledge and love of the migrants require pushing one's borders beyond the boundaries leading to relationship and acceptance. It involves solidarity with the marginalized communities with a commitment to seek justice together. It is a dialogical journey of partners in the kingdom spirituality overcoming fear and shame, more so with those living under the fear of deportation, erasing one's very personhood. Such a commitment of solidarity and collaboration can confer identity to those living under the fear of detainment and deportation. True solidarity is built on the plenitude of love.

Multiculturalism has become a household term in most countries, but what has not been equally understood is that ethnicity has taken on a new role. As Vincenzo Cesareo has argued convincingly, ethnicity has become a cultural vehicle through which to project needs, demands and requirements linked to widely differing patterns of life. "Ethnic identity no longer refers exclusively to traditional elements of an ascribed type, but accentuates the cultural dimension and is often used to furnish the group with idioms and symbols in order to claim rights, in a context in which the deed for identity (and for the recognition of different identities) erupts in a crisis of meaning in a general process of social atomism."[20] Ethnicity can be interwoven with interests, capable of stirring up polemics and political mobilization. However, this in itself need not become a deterrent for Christian reaching out to migrants of differing ethnicities.

Global migration as we experience it, has to be seen as part of the ongoing divine revelation in our history and we are invited to respond to it. Our answer to it with Christian response-ability will help to transform the existing identities of powerlessness and marginalization as "no people," to usher in an identity of equality and partnership. By doing that, Christian communities in the host countries will become the incarnational presence of God in our history, in our language and in our events. It is ongoing salvation history and is integral to the understanding of the world as a sacrament of encounter with God. As Vatican II's Pastoral Constitution, church in the Modern World, articulated, Christians "try to discern the true sign of God's presence and purpose in the events, the needs and desires which it shares with the rest of humanity today" (n.11).

Mission as God's reaching out can liberate the secular energies of the gospels when it is not, primarily at least, associated with religion. Jesus and his message is very much part of day to day human living: as a friend of the tax collectors and sinners, nicknamed as a glutton and a drunkard, who preferred celebration to fasting, Jesus moved in the secular space rather than the sacred. Except on special occasions like the cleansing of the temple, we meet him at common meals with ordinary people. Jesus was the incarnation of the eternal divine hospitality, the unfailing divine welcome.

All these are challenges for the Christian community in its dealing with migrants. Like Jesus, the local Christian community has to overcome the tendency to be exclusive in its identity based on race, country, or other anthropological and religious considerations. It has to denounce violence in any form, humiliation, rejection or silencing, all of which are common experiences of migrants in different degrees. Perceiving their vulnerability and disempowerment, the Christian community is constantly reminding itself of its obligation to re-present the divine hospitality by making itself a home to the migrants. Gemma Tulud Cruz underlines how home is an aspirational aspect of Jesus' ministry, "a place and space where justice is done and respect and compassion unite everyone."[21] It becomes a model to be unaffected by the colour, or fear of migrants, and to foster connectivity and relationship, in words, actions and body language.

The grim reality that migrants face in economic pressures, lack of emotional support structures, discord, violence, demands of adjusting to the new culture, language, all compound their vulnerability. This cannot be evaded but challenges Christians to do everything possible to assuage an intolerant situation. Christian churches have started a process of building social awareness both within the Christian community and in civil society of issues related to migration and the benefits of having diversity in cultures and religions.

Based on his study of the work of Fr. Pawlicki, a Polish American missionary among the Mexican immigrants in Coachella in southern California, Daniel Groody points out how love has to be at the heart of mission to the migrants, with attentiveness to what migrants have lived through.[22]

Frequently many migrants, despite their helping the families back home, go through up-rootedness, isolation with the accompanying stress and loneliness. The church can give them a sense of belonging and oneness with the rest of the society. The church is not just an organizing and helping body, leaving the migrants in their mute anonymity. Rather, prompted by Christian love, it encourages a form of involvement and participation, and this in turn, hastens the process of the emerging new identity as the local church, leaving behind the painful experiences of loneliness, marginalization and meaninglessness. Migrants find not simply places of spiritual service but homes of welcome. True, it is a struggle for the church as well, to overcome the tendency to see immigrants fit only as people to fill jobs at the lowest sector of society without fully accepting them as members of society.

The emerging multicultural identity includes also a sensibility and openness to different Christian traditions as well as to non Christian traditions that sustain the soul of the migrants in the midst of all their woes. Both ecumenism and the 'wider ecumenism,' more so at the grass-root level, are vibrant among most Catholics.

Concluding Remarks

The contemporary experience of migration must remind us, as Robert Schreiter has called our attention to, that "the migration stories of the Hebrew Scriptures are often the sites where God's revelation takes place and God's grace is revealed."[23] Aware of how human mobility is a leading mark of our times the Christian community unfolds its mission as "an epiphany of God's will and the fulfilment of that will in the world and in world history" (*Ad Gentes* n.9), and, thus, becomes an expression of the *extensio Dei*, God's welcoming and accepting presence for the migrants, who are to a large extent "sheep without a shepherd," empowering them to have a new identity in a multicultural society, enjoying acceptance and appreciation along with the recognition of the identity of others – identity with alterity.

Endnotes

[1] Clerk Clarke S, Manchala D, and Peacok, *Dalit Theology in the Twenty-first Century Discordant Voices (Discerning Pathways,* Oxford: University Press, 2010), 9.

[2] M. Abella, "Migration in the World Today," *Sedos Bulletin* Vol 37 no 5/6, (2005):103.

[3] Abella, "Migration in the World Today,": 102.

[4] World Council of Churches, "Consultation on Mission and Ecclesiology of the Migrant Churches" *International Review of Mission* 100.1 (2011):104.

[5] Un.org/development/desa/en/news/population/international_migrant_stock_2019.html

[6] Katalina Tahaafe-Williams, "Multicultural Ministry: A Call to Act Justly," *International Review of Mission,* 1001.1 (2011):21.

[7] Gerrit Noort, "Emerging Migrant Churches in the Netherlands: Missiological Challenges and Mission Frontiers," *International Review of Mission,* 100.1, (2011): 5.

[8] http://www.bbc.co.uk/news/business_16305048.

[9] Graziano Battistella, "What Protection for Migrants? Migration Policies and Human Rights," *Sedos Bulletin* Vol 37, 11-12 (2005):204.

[10] Abella, "Migration in the World Today," *Sedos Bulletin*:106.

[11] For instance, in recent times three Indian immigrants to the US won Nobel prizes: Gobind Khurana, Chadra Shekar and V Ramakrishna, which tells something about the US identity in general.

[12] S Lefebvre and Susin (eds), *Migration in a Global World* (London: SCM Press, 2008), 8.

[13] Final Statement of the Seventh Plenary Assembly of the Federation of the Asian Bishops' Conferences, in Franz Josef Eilers (ed), *For All the Peoples of Asia. Federation of Asian Bishops' Conferences Documents from 2002 to 2006,* Vol 3 (Quezon City: Claretian Publications 2006), 11.

[14] Richard Lucien, *Living the Hospitality of God* (New York: Paulist Press, 2000).

[15] G. Newlands & A. Smith, *Hospitality of God: The Transformative Dream* (London: Ashgate, 2010).

[16] Newlands & Smith, *Hospitality of God,* 217.

[17] Newlands & Smith, *Hospitality of God,* vii.

[18] Paulo Suess, "Missio Dei and the Project of Jesus: The Poor and the "other" as the Mediators of the Kingdom and Protagonists of the Churches," *Sedos Bulletin* Vol 44, No1/2 (2012):3.

[19] Ibid.

[20] Vincenzo Cesareo, "Integration into an Intercultural World: Christian Proposal for a United Society," *Sedos Bulletin Vol 37 n 9/10,* (2005):161.

[21] Gemma Tulud Cruz, "Expanding the Boundaries, Turning Borders into Spaces: Mission in the Context of Contemporary Migration," in Kalu U Vethanayagamony & E Chia, (eds) Luisville: WJK, 2010, 83.

[22] Daniel Groody, "The Mission of the Church with Migrants Today" *Sedos Bulletin,* Vol 37 no 5/6 (2005):148.

[23] Robert Schreiter, "Catholicity as a Framework for Addressing Migration," *Concilium* n.5 (2008):34.

Chapter - 6

Fresh Perspectives on Inter Religious Dialogue in Relation to Christian Mission

Arguably most Christians have come to the conviction that dialogue with the followers of other religious traditions is integral to Christian mission in modern times, as manifested in the surge in theological literature on Inter Religious Dialogue (IRD). Most of the time, however, it reflects either a spirit of Christian superiority, or an attitude of resignation, "since, nothing else is possible." On the other hand, our age, with its prevailing reality of globalization accompanied by instant communication and mass migration, has effected, in many respects, a vision of one world along with its characteristic religious pluralism.[1] Equally, we experience also the dividing walls of violence of many shades, poverty and injustice. This is a great challenge for Christians in the context of their call to be witnesses of the good news of Jesus Christ, "the arrival of the acceptable year of the Lord" (Lk 4:19). This chapter argues how the Christian response to this context is engagement in IRD as the expression of Christian participation in God's self-reaching out in love and this, in fact, has to become the primary way of Christian mission today.

The Good News

Though the four evangelists differ in their perspectives, they converge in their presentation of the good news. Mark the first one to write the gospel, begins by stating how the good news began to be (1.1) and how it comes to be continued (16:7), with the description of the ministry in between. The ministry itself is the focal point and it is a narrative of how through his ministry Jesus ushers in the divine reign (1:14-15). Mathew concurs with Mark by repeating almost the same words (4:17). Luke, the evangelist whose purpose was to make a "systematic narration of the events" (1:3), dwells on how God's reign is brought on earth by Jesus (4:18-21). In the second part of the Lukan narrative, the Acts of the Apostles, Peter summarizes the entire mission of Jesus as "going about doing good" (10:38). The fourth evangelist though sparse in the use of the terminology of the divine reign, nevertheless, is faithful to the reality in so far as he states that the mission of Jesus was manifesting the deeds of light, "that it may be clearly seen that his deeds have been wrought in God (3:21, 16-21).

Jesus began his ministry by proclaiming the arrival of the acceptable of year of the Lord, which was good news to the poor. Jesus, above all, had an intimate experience of God that others did not have, and this he tried to share with all, with his followers and with others, with all its implications, being compassionate to one another, leading to communion. The salvation that Jesus spoke about was a transformation of life on earth with right relationship with the neighbour and with God (see, Lk 10:25-37; 19:1-10; Mt 25:31-46, and others).

Later Developments

Though Jesus' primary message was good news to the poor, he spelt it out through the prophetic words of Isaiah 61.1-2, sight to the blind, ability to walk to the lame, setting at liberty the captives - in one word - concern for the neighbour (Mt 25:31-40). The religious system transformed it into a discourse of heaven and hell, punishment and reward, an after-death reality. Works like *Cur Deus Homo?* (Why God became a Man, Anselm of Canterbury, completed in 1098), advocating satisfaction/atonement as the justification for the Incarnation, contributed to a radical deviation of church's life and mission. What initially was the Way (Act 11:26) and the Kingdom-movement, becomes the sanctuary of the eternally saved. Christian mission was primarily to bring as many as possible into the church. Salvation itself was interpreted as an otherworldly reality that can be gained only within the church. Christianity thus became a "universalizing religion,"[2] with the Christians proclaiming that their religion alone possessed religious truth and that "the world would be a better place if everyone belonged to them."[3]

The Christian Call

Since the middle of the twentieth century, there began to be a change. As far as the Catholics are concerned Vatican II made a corrective move by insisting how all have a common origin and a common destiny (NA 1) and exhorted Catholics to enter prudently and lovingly into dialogue with followers of other religions and thus "acknowledge, preserve, and promote the spiritual and moral goods found among these men, as well as the values in their society and culture" (NA 2). In this, the Council was only upholding the biblical revelation that affirms the creation of all humans by God into God's own image and with whom God entered into an eternal covenant (Gen 1.26-

28). Evangelist John made this vision as the opening theme of the gospel. The word, through whom God created all and who enlightens all, became flesh (1:1-4, 9). All revelation and religious knowledge is traced to the same mystery. Equally, all salvation is through the same mystery. There is no reason to make a distinction between natural and supernatural revelation and natural and revealed religions, in so far as every religious activity is the response to the same revealing mystery. Jonathan Sacks, a leading thinker of contemporary times, has counselled, "There is more than one way of being-in-the-world under the sovereignty of God."[4]

However, the Bible insists equally how right from the beginning God calls individuals and peoples for a specific service. Thus, Abraham is called to become a blessing to all (Gen 12:3). In the same spirit Israel is called to serve as a light to the nations (Is 42:6; 49:6). In fact, right before God makes the covenant with Israel, they are told that they are made his people so that they are to be a kingly, priestly and holy nation (Ex 19:5-6). All the three roles remind them of their vocation to be of service to the rest of the nations.[5]

This same call is continued through the formation (creation)[6] of the new community of the disciples of Jesus Christ. The Matthean inaugural sermon unmistakably points to their service as the salt and light to the world (Mt 5:13-16). Even the post-resurrection mission mandate is linked to this role, by including the teaching of "all that I have commanded you" (Mt 28:20). There have to be communities of disciples of Jesus in every culture precisely for serving as the salt, light and leaven (Mt 5:13-14). Hence the message of the kingdom is accompanied by the creation of the new community (Mk 1:15-20; 3:13-14). This role of the Christian community today, as the Vatican Council declared, is fulfilled through IRD. Not only the Catholic church, but the other churches too made IRD a priority.[7]

In the past Christian theology, in general, was trying to explain away other religions, with the theories of preparation, fulfilment, seeds of the Word, etc., always holding that Christianity is the only God-willed religion.[8] Today Christians have to ask themselves as to what is the service that they can render to a world in which God is actively involved, but always keeping in mind the Christian call to service. The church now regards with esteem the believers of all religions, appreciating their moral and spiritual commitment. As Pope Francis has pointed out, "there have been so many events, initiatives, institutional or personal relationships with non-Christian religions in these fifty years, since the publication of *Nostra Aetate*."[9] The Pope characterized these as expressions of the church's hope that all believers in God would favour friendship and unity between peoples. Indifference and opposition have changed to collaboration and benevolence. "Former enemies and strangers, we have become friends and brothers."[10]

Christian call does not adopt a "one-among-the many" attitude, but the call is to follow the word incarnate in his mission of realizing the divine reign. As John Paul II wrote to Cardinal Cassidy on the occasion of the XIII International Meeting of Peoples and Religion, "we must all be bolder on this journey, so that the men and women of our world, to whatever people or belief they belong, can discover that they are children of the one God and brothers and sisters to one another."[11]

The Christian call, according to Pope Francis, is to be "missionary disciples" (*The Joy of the Gospel* 120). However, this does not mean that Christians reach out to the followers of other religions only as raw material for church growth, but as collaborators in realizing the divine reign. Christian call is not to proselytize, but respect others' beliefs and, thus, inspire others through Christian witness so as to grow together through communication. In this the Christian community has an important role to serve as the leaven.

Inter Religious Dialogue

IRD is not an entity but a process of becoming. It is a process of becoming a community of persons, respectful and respecting, transforming and transformed, renewing and renewed. This allows the process of IRD a certain amount of spontaneity as well as open- endedness. It acknowledges the need to turn to each other and together to the ground of our being, to the goal of our existence. Thus, it is permeated by a sense of the radical transcendence and at the same time down to earth immanence in so far as it is primarily directed to the horizontal level of understanding and acceptance. It is through and through guided by the mandate to "seek first the divine reign" (Mt 6:33). IRD is a cooperative and constructive interaction among people belonging to different religious traditions[12] leading to communion.

IRD is a symbol of the kingdom, to which we are pilgrimaging: it is a "diffuse symbol"[13] (Gerald A. Arbuckle), i.e., its meaning depends on the different contexts of the dialogue process: faith, religion, and commitment to transformation:

Leading to a religiously experienced meaning. After all, symbol is an embodiment of meaning, enabling humans to communicate, perpetuate and develop a vision of human life.

Symbol has the innate ability to make us feel 'at home'. At the same time, by the same logic, it invites us to enter into the world of the symbols of the other and this is the mystery of, the dynamic of IRD, ushering in the gifts of different faiths that will serve as a reservoir of common pilgrimage – the reality of IRD.

A symbol is any reality that by its very dynamism or power leads to another deeper reality through a sharing in the dynamism that the symbol itself offers (and merely by verbal or additional explanations.)[14]

A good many of modern problems and conflicts, strangely though, have religion at their root,[15] whether it is the Arab-Israel conflict, conflicts in the Middle East and Syria, the Kashmir problem, Indonesian conflicts, the conflicts in the southern Philippines and many others. In theory, practically all religions have the inbuilt theological underpinning for mutual understanding and collaboration. The belief in the *antaryamin* in Hinduism[16], i.e., the Divine indwells in all human beings, the Islamic vision of all humans by nature making a self-surrender to God, the Buddhist teaching of universal compassion, the Christian call to love and care for the neighbour, the basic understanding of harmony in the Chinese and Confucian religions, the understanding of Yahweh, the creator of all and as the Lord of History in Judaism, the vision of the salvation of the universe as understood by the primal religions, are all inviting religions to come closer and to collaborate, rather than to compete and combat with each other. Right relationship with neighbours is the focus of all religions. This is the challenge of inter religious dialogue. Christians in particular, by their call to witness to the coming of the divine reign in Jesus Christ, the Incarnation of the *extensio Dei,* are called to IRD.

Prophet Isaiah's vision, 6:1-8, reminds us how our history, our experience of God, does not begin with us. The history of all people of God is part of our intimate relationship with God. "All the earth is filled with his glory" (Is 6:3). Isaiah's vision tells us also that no one, not even Isaiah or Moses, can have a total vision of the divine and this is an invitation for religions to touch the Holy as experienced in the other, to be enriched by the other. God's dialogue with humans does not begin with any particular religion but with creation. The Bible insists also on a universal covenant of God with humans (Gen 9:9-17).

This is a challenge for all followers of the different religious traditions to look into what they have in common rather than what differentiates them. It has to be acknowledged how all religions advocate peace, love, unity and tolerance, which in the past, due to narrow missionary zeal, was overlooked. Equally, there is no room to compare religions in order to establish one's own superiority. As the Benedictine nun and author, Joan Chittister, has underlined no people is unique in an absolute sense, in so far as anything in human condition is common to all. "And all of these peoples have grappled with the same kinds of questions and have arrived at their own answers."[17] What is important is to realize how each religion has a particular service to render to humanity, and ask how together we can usher in a superior quality of human existence.

Already the Old Testament paves the way for inter religious understanding leading to enrichment of one's religion. The Babylonian exile brought Israel into contact with the leading religion of the Babylonian world, Zoroastrianism and to be enriched by it, in the understanding of notion of one God. We come across strict monotheism in the Bible only towards the end of the exile (Is 45:18) though there was already the monolatry. The Zoroastrian understanding of the two ages facilitated the belief in the idea of resurrection of the dead. Sean Freyne writes: "The doctrine of the two ages is the theological underpinning for the belief in the idea of the resurrection of the dead – a doctrine that finds its first unequivocal expression in Daniel: 12:2-3".[18] Judaism's adaptation to a life without the temple through the institution of the synagogue, too, results from the Zoroastrians who did not have one central temple but a temple where a community existed.[19]

In the gospels, as we have seen already, Jesus is not an advocate of a religion as much as a quality of life based on love and mercy. The early Christians were quite creative in their openness and sensitivity to the religious world of the times manifested in doing away with circumcision (Acts 15), in the theological interpretation of Jesus as the Lord rather than as Christ/Messiah (Acts 11:20 in contrast to Acts 9:22), and in similar theological and practical developments.

Christian Service

The Christian call stands in continuity with the call of Israel as a chosen people, to serve humanity as a kingly, priestly and holy nation (Ex 19: 6). This was repeated by Jesus in his sermon on the mount by reminding the community of his disciples that they are to serve the world as its light (Mt 5:14) and salt (5:13) (Cf also 1 Pt 2:9). The Christian community is the continuation of the **ministry** of the incarnate word (Jn 20:21) who creates and enlightens all humans coming into the world (Jn 1:1-4, 9). The Christian community is aware, on the one hand, of the presence of the divine in all humans, on the other, and at the same time, it realizes how it has a service to render to humanity, as the sacrament of the divine reign. Today this can be realized primarily, not exclusively, through IRD. To quote Jurgen Moltmann, "The church's abiding origin in Israel, its permanent orientation to Israel's hope, Christianity's resulting special vocation to prepare the way for the coming kingdom in history – all this will also give its stamp to the dialogue with the world religions."[20]

Even as Jesus was anointed by the spirit to bring the good news to the poor, so also the Christian call is to be an agent of the good news to the poor (Mk 3:14-15; Lk 24:48-49; Mt 5:13-15 and Jn 20:21). What is required is a return to Jesus' own (God's own) priorities. This, in today's world, can be done only in collaboration with all. That is what makes IRD the fulcrum of the church's service to the world today.

Scientists tell us how we have entered a new geological epoch, that of the Anthropocene, i.e., human actions affecting the very metabolism of the planet postponing the next ice age at least by 50,000 years.[21] This makes the care of the earth, as our very immediate neighbour, also very much part of the realization of the acceptable year of the Lord. Pope Francis made care of the earth a central concern of the Catholic Church and invites followers of all religions "to dialogue among themselves for the sake of protecting nature, defending the poor, and building networks of respect and fraternity. … The gravity of the ecological crisis demands that we all look to the common good, embarking on a path of dialogue which demands patience, self-discipline and generosity, always keeping in mind that "realities are greater than ideas."[22]

In IRD Christians work united in their common humanity and mutual responsibility, as well as in the shared values and convictions. In this Christians, as the expression of their service to the realization of the acceptable year of the Lord, can and must take the lead to foster a culture of human ecology that increasingly promotes harmony within individuals and in their relationships. The community of the disciples, the little flock (Lk

12:32), has to become the leaven and light in this movement of IR collaboration.

Christian commitment invites Christians to appreciate the fact that every culture and every religion is a manifestation of divine love and goodness, though mixed also with human selfishness. It is here that a Christian sees the significance of the healing mission of Jesus with his message of the kingdom. Any local Christian community anywhere in the world must enter into dialogue with local religions as the continuation of the Lord Jesus' ministry. This made the Evangelical churches to affirm in their October 2010 Cape Town Commitment: "In the name of the God of love, we repent of our failure to seek friendships with people of Muslim, Hindu, Buddhist and other religious backgrounds. In the spirit of Jesus, we will take initiatives to show love, goodwill and hospitality to them."[23]

Metaphysical Humility

Christians cannot play God or dictate terms to God by asking God to do "homework" (Kosuke Koyama), restrict God's salvation only to those whom Christians recommend, but allow themselves to be subject to God's plans. This requires a metaphysical humility that acknowledges Christian limitations and the perfectibility of their religious tradition and their understanding of it, as well as the religious truth to which others respond prompted by the Mystery of the same Word that became flesh (Jn 1:9). As Catherine Cornille has suggested, this humility is motivated also by "the recognition of the partial and finite nature of the ways in which ultimate truth has been grasped and expressed in the teachings and practices of one's own tradition."[24] Obviously, such humility demands the giving up of claims of ultimate and exclusive monopoly over truth and revelation in so far as it can only lead to interreligious conflicts and violence, not to speak of the fact that the Bible does not always support such claims.

Raymond Panikkar has spoken of the need to have an ontological humility in interreligious dialogue in so far as dialogue reminds all of their temporality, contingency, and their constitutive limitation. "Humility is not primarily a moral virtue, but an ontological one; it is the awareness of the place of my ego, the truthfulness of accepting my real situation, namely, that I am a situated being, a vision's angle on the real of the real, an existence."[25] Such a metaphysical humility enabled mystics like Abhishiktananda and Bede Griffiths to be enriched by entering into the very soul of Hinduism. Abhishiktananda was the first Catholic Priest to sit at the feet of a Hindu guru making himself a disciple of Sri Ramana Maharsi. This enabled Abhishiktananda to realize that the great primitive Upananishads, like the Chandogya and Brihadaranyaka, are the incomparable witness to the awakening of the soul to the Mystery of being and of the self, and these earliest formulations of that experience have never been surpassed.[26]

Historical Consciousness

History, the time in which we live, is not just a succession of events, a chronology, but it is very much part of God's plan for us, in which God acts. Thus, it is very much a *Kairos*, divine time (salvation history). Christians through their involvement in IRD are called to collaborate in the divine design to convert chronos into Kairos.

The late Pope John XXIII expressed this historical consciousness through his pointing out the need to read "the signs of the times"[27] which can be characterized as the ongoing divine revelation in history. The spring time of religious revival that we witness everywhere may be said to be a sign of the time in this sense and has to be taken seriously as long as it enables humans to grow in love and concern for each other.

All religions must build bridges among themselves based on the inter connectedness of the understanding of the ultimate reality, despite differences in the specific grasp and explanation of the same. Today scholars like David Tracy and Francis Clooney speak of comparative theology, a theology developed not only on the basis of one's own scriptures but also in the light of one's reading of the scriptures of other religions.[28] It underlines the need for thinking inter-religiously, interpreting home tradition in critical correlation with other traditions.

Similarly, there has to be a certain amount of willingness to place oneself into the religious world of the other, not only intellectually by trying to understand the reality behind the religious symbols of the other, but also through an honest attempt to enter into the religious mind set of the other with a view to understand the other from within. Catherine Cornille expresses it well: "Even though religion is certainly more than a feeling, the affective dimension does play a crucial role in the religious life of any person, and a proper understanding of another religion would thus be seriously impoverished with access to the meaning of a particular belief or practice for the person involved."[29] Religions would require empathy to enter into relationship and communion with one another.

Witnessing to Jesus Christ

Empathy for one another will lead the followers of religious traditions to certain reciprocity in dialogue, sharing their religious experience with an openness to understand each other's faith. It is here that the Christian will witness to Jesus Christ, making it clear that what makes the Christian be involved in inter religious dialogue is precisely in response to Jesus' call to collaborate in ringing in the divine reign. This is a significant form of mission in the post-colonial era. Obviously, we can pray and hope that at least some, with whom we enter into dialogue, may be attracted to Jesus Christ and commit themselves to follow him in his ministry without ruling out the possibility of the dialogue partner too having similar desires. At any rate, mission in the post-colonial world is not any more a one way traffic but a sharing of one's spiritual experience with others.

Dialogue, more so intellectual dialogue, generally presupposes a certain level of informational exchange and the growth of knowledge about the dialogue partner's faith. This in turn, can lead to some sort of mutual religious fecundation, reciprocal inspiration and transformation. Interreligious dialogue, thus, becomes the context of witnessing, open to various possibilities that are to be left to the receiver and to divine inspiration. However, in interreligious dialogue there is no question of any one-sided prophetic dialogue, nor is interreligious dialogue as such aimed at winning the dialogue partner to one's own religion. Interreligious dialogue is a dialogue in bold humility.

However, the Christian partner enters into dialogue as part of his/her commitment to follow Jesus Christ in his mission of making God's presence concrete and tangible in the world (Mt. 1:23 Jn 12:45), by becoming other-centred and working for the wholeness of life for all, as Jesus did. Similarly, the World Council of Churches in its *Guidelines on Dialogue* (1979) asserts: "Dialogue, therefore, is a fundamental part of Christian service within community. In dialogue Christians actively respond to the command to "love God and your neighbour as yourself. As an expression of love engagement dialogue testifies to the love experienced in Christ" (n 18). What is required is a historicization of the call of the World Council of Churches as well as Vatican II. As Massimo Faggioli, an expert in Vatican II wrote: "One of the ever-growing and important elements of Vatican II is the practical implications of *ressourcement* and *rapprochement* – "deepening" and "reaching out," "reconciliation by proximity."[30] Each religion has kerygmatic as well as mystical aspects though some religions may emphasise one over the other.[31] Christianity is a combination of both these aspects especially in the fourth gospel. God reveals to humans from outside calling for transformation. Christianity tries to live this call. Simultaneously, as Gerd Theissen has shown there is, particularly in the fourth gospel, with its claim for absoluteness with boundless love, there is the mystical tradition as well.[32] Theissen has emphasized how "this Gospel of love must be seen as the only thing which is absolute in religious dialogue."[33]

IRD is a theologically loaded process of understanding and exercising Christian mission as a participation in God's self-reaching out. Through IRD Christian community becomes a communication of the good news of the divine reign, refraining from anything that is religiously divisive or fundmentalistic. Pope Francis reminds us how IRD is a "new form of missionary creativity," (*Amoris Laetitiae* 57), Summoning all Christians "to revive our hope and make it a source of prophetic visions, transformative actions and creative focus of charity" (AL 57).

Conversion and IRD

Engagement in IRD can get bogged down with the issue of conversion.[34] As we have seen conversion, understood as a transformation, is integral to IRD. For the Vatican Document, *Dialogue and Mission* "conversion is the humble and penitent return of the heart to God in the desire to submit one's life more generously to him."[35] In this sense conversion is central to IRD, even as it is part of the daily life of any one as a process of maturation.

Biblically understood, conversion is a return (*shub* in Hebrew) to the originary relational situation of harmony and communion with God and with one another (Ps 51:13; Ps 19:7; Is 1:27, etc.). Jesus's summon to conversion in the context of the arrival of the divine reign was in tune with this biblical spirit manifested in his teachings (Mt 5:38-48; 7:1-5, Lk 10:29ff., 18:23ff., etc.).

The deeper commitment to God, normally, is through the religion to which one belongs, though the possibility cannot be ruled out that one becomes convinced that the dialogue partner's religion is the God-intended religion for that person, thus, leading to a change – conversion - from one religion to another. However, proselytization from one religion to another is not the intent of IRD. Rather, Christian initiative of IRD is also an admission that the Christian community has new perceptions with regard to proselytization. As the World Council of Churches' Guidelines on Dialogue with People of Living Faiths and Ideologies stated, "Dialogue in community is not a secret weapon in the armoury of an aggressive Christian militancy. Rather it is a means of living our faith in Christ in service of community with one's neighbours" (n 18). IRD invites the dialoguing partners, in contrast to conquering, displacing, competing, mere tolerating or co-existence, to communication, collaboration and exchange motivated by the respect for the religious identity of the other.

Concluding Remarks

At its earliest stage Christian mission was a sharing of an experience (1Jn 1:1-4), without any reference to any fall or atonement. It continued in that spirit until the time of the emperor Constantine and the imperial conquests thereafter. Gradually mission becomes merged with political motives and this process reaches its climax during the colonial days, fanned by the Anselmian atonement theology, when mission was understood exclusively as an engagement with the followers of other religions - mission *ad gentes*. Post colonialism brings the challenge to return to the original kingdom-centred mission that requires a mission along with and in collaboration with the followers of other religions - mission *inter-Religiones*. In this process the Christian community has to play a constructive and vital role due to their commitment to follow Jesus Christ, *extensio Dei*. Apart from this proactive impulse to IRD, the Christian community has to ensure that it does not contribute in any way to the religious madness and violence fuelled by religious sentiments that one comes across in many parts of the world. As the Interreligious Consultation, jointly organized by the Pontifical Council for Interreligious Dialogue and the Office for Interreligious Relations and Dialogue of the World Council of Churches and participated also by representatives of other religions, stated: "All of us believe that religions should be a source of uniting and ennobling of humans. Religions, understood and practiced in the light of the core principles and ideals of each of our faiths, can be a reliable guide to meeting the many challenges before humankind."[36] IRD is the golden rule for Christians today – transcend to transform!

Endnotes

[1] Sociologist Peter L. Berger has pointed out pluralism is an ideology, whereas the reality is plurality. (see, Peter L. Berger, "The Good of Religious Pluralism," in *First Things* (April 2016), 40.

[2] Rita M. Gross, "Models of Religious Belonging," in *Religious Conversion: Religion Scholars Thinking Together*, Shanta Premawardhana (ed), (West Sussex, UK: Wiley Blackwell, 2015), 33.

[3] Ibid, 35.

[4] Jonathan Sacks, *Not in God's Name: Confronting Religious Violence*, London: Hodder, 2016, 99.

[5] Cf. Blackburn, W. Ross, *The God who Makes himself Known: The missionary heart of the Book of Exodus* (Downers Grove, Il: Inter Varsity Press, 2012), 89-95.

[6] In the Greek original the evangelist Mark uses the verb *epoiesen* (3:14), the same verb that is used in Genesis 1.1, and in both instances, it means created/made.

[7] World Council of Churches, *Guidelines on Dialogue with People of Living Faiths and Ideologies* (Geneva: WCC, 1979).

[8] See Alan Race, *Christians and Religious Pluralism* (Maryknoll, NY: Orbis Books, 1982).

[9] Pope Francis, Inter Religious Dialogue: Address to the General Audience Wednesday, 28 October 2015. http//www.wa.vatican.va/Francesco/en/audences/2015/documents/pope-francesco_20151028_udienza-generale. Html (accessed on 26-01-2016)

[10] Ibid.

[11] John Paul II, "Message to Cardinal Cassidy," *Pro Dialogo 106/1(2001)*:12.

[12] See Terry C. Muck, "Missio-logoi, interreligious dialogue, and the parable of the Good Samaritan," *Missiology*, 44/1 (2016):8.

[13] Gerald Arbuckle, *Culture, Inculturation, Theology* (Collegeville, MI: Michael Glacier, 2010), 25.

[14] Ibid.

[15] See Jonathan Sacks, *Not in God's Name: Confronting Religious Violence.*

[16] According to Rg Veda Reality is one but sages name it differently (*ekam sat: vipra bahudah vdanti*) (Rg 1.164.46).

[17] Joan Chittister, *Welcome to the Wisdom of the World: Universal Spiritual Insights from five Religious Traditions*, (Grand Rapids, MI: W. B. Eerdmans, 2007), xi.

[18] Freyne Sean, *The world of the New Testament*, (Wilmington, Del: Michael Glazier, 1983), 95.

[19] Though one hardly comes across scholarly literature stating that the synagogue worship rose due to the influence of Zoroastrianism, scholars like Martin A. Cohen do recognize how the synagogue originated during the Babylonian captivity in the 6th century BCE (Cf. Martin A. Cohen, "Synagogue," *The Encyclopaedia of Religions*. Vol 14, (New York: McMillan, 1987: 209-218), and this in turn supports Freyne Sean's position that the Jewish synagogue came into being under the influence of Zoroastrianism (Sean. 1983, 96).

[20] Jurgen Moltmann, *The Church in the Power of the Spirit* (London: SCM Press, 1977), 150.

[21] Science and Environment, BBC.com/news/science-environment-35307800. Accessed on 14-01-2016.

[22] Pope Francis, *Laudato Si* (Vatican: Vatican Press, 2015), n 201.

[23] "The Cape Town Commitment: A Confession of Faith and a Call to Action," *International Bulletin of Missionary Research*, Vol 35, No.2 (April 2011):72.

[24] Catherine Cornille, *The Impossibility of Interreligious Dialogue* (New York: The Crossroad Publishing Company, 2008), 10.

[25] Raimon Panikkar, *Intra Religious Dialogue* (New York: Paulist Press, 1999), 37.

[26] Swami Abhishiktananda, *Hindu-Christian Meeting Point* (Bangalore: CISRS, 1969), 51.

[27] John XXIII, *Apostolic Constitution "Humane Salutis,"* December 25, 1961 in Walter M Abbott, (ed) *Documents of Vatican II* (New York: Guild Press, 1966), 704.

[28] David Tracy, "Comparative Theology," *Encyclopaedia of Religions, Vol 13*, Lindsy Jones (ed), 2nd edn, Detroit: Macmillan, 2005, 9125-34; Francis Clooney, *Comparative Theology: Deep Learning Across Religious Borders* (West Sussexx, UK: Wiley Blackwell), 2010.

[29] Catherine Cornille, *The Impossibility of Interreligious Dialogue, 138.*

[30] Faggioli, Massimo, *A Council for the Global Church: Receiving Vatican II in History* (Minneapolis, MN: Fortress Press, 2015), 176.

[31] Cf. Johannes Nissen, *The Gospel of John and the Religious Quest: Historical and Contemporary Perspectives* (Eugene, Or: Pickwich Publications, 2013), 190.

[32] Gerd Theissen, *Lichtspuren. Predigten und Bibelarbeiten,* (Guetersloh: Kaiser, 1994), 156-158. Cf. J. Nissen, *The Gospel of John,* 71.

[33] Gerd Theissen, *Lichtspuren,* 161. Quoted in Nissen, *The Gospel of John, 191.*

[34] See, for instance, the Inter-Religious Consultation on Conversion organized by the PCID and WCC, Lariano (Italy) May 12-16, 2006 in "Report from Inter-Religious Consultation on Conversion," (http://www. Oikoumene.org/en/resources/documents/wcc/-programmes/interreligious-dialogue-and-cooperation, accessed on 06/02/2016).

[35] Secretariat for Non-Christians, *The Attitude of the Church Towards the Followers of Other Religions*, Vatican City, Pentecost 1984, no 37.

[36] WCC. *Current Dialogue*, Issue 47, June 2006. (http:// wcc-coc.org/wcc/ what/interreligious/cd47-18.html), accessed on 24/02/2016.

Chapter - 7

Reformation, Ecumenism and Mission Today

The year 2017 was the five hundredth anniversary of the Reformation that Martin Luther gave rise to. It almost coincided with the fiftieth anniversary of the great Ecumenical Council Vatican II. Triggered by that confluence, this chapter argues how the double celebration must help the church to retrieve the roots and fruits of Christian discipleship from the ministry of Jesus Christ.

The quincentennial commemoration of the reformation movement is an invitation to revisit some of the principles that Luther emphasised and which are also basic to Christian faith. The course of events and developments that have transpired during the past five centuries as well as the distance in time enable one to review what Luther said with certain equanimity but also with a view to enrich the church's life and mission for the contemporary times.

As Hans Kung has pointed out[1] the Reformation may be attributed to several persons and factors though basically it was Luther who initiated the event by his questioning of the church's granting indulgence, that is, remittance of punishment due to a dead person, in return for the money a living person gives to the church. The conflict concerning the indulgences developed into a question of spiritual authority which Luther understood in terms of the scripture.[2]

The five hundred-year anniversary of the Reformation must prove to be an event strengthening ecumenism, eventually paving the way for the unity of the church. "Commitment to ecumenism responds to the prayer of the Lord Jesus that 'they be one' (Jn 17:21)," wrote Pope Francis in his Apostolic Exhortation *Evangelii Gaudium* (The Joy of the Gospel) (no 214). The Pope went on to say: "The credibility of the Christian message would be much greater if Christians could overcome their divisions and the church could realize the fullness of catholicity proper to her."

In the same spirit the Pope in his address to the Ecumenical event in Malmo Arena, Sweden on 31 October 2016, remembering the 500 anniversary of the Reformation, said: "We remember this anniversary with a renewed spirit and in the recognition that Christian Unity is a priority, because we realize that much more unites us than separates us."[3] In this the Pope is only following one of the leading guidelines of Vatican II saying that the church of Christ has to be unique and one (*Unitatis Redintegratio* 1).

Charting that path of ecumenism, this chapter will argue how the Catholic Church can draw inspiration from Luther to make the church ever more missionary, especially with regard to the role of the Laity as outlined by Vatican II. Reformation and Vatican II together invite all Christians to have a ministry-centred approach to the Lord as presented in the gospels.

Significance of Ecumenism

It is widely recognized how the world at large is changing in interactions and collaborations, tending to greater unity, despite the fissiparous tendencies fostered by narrow-minded vested interests. This has not left the Christian churches unaffected as shown by the many joint study groups and inter-ecclesial commissions to usher in greater unity among Christians. The ecumenical ideal is upheld by all churches, more so by the Catholic Church, the World Council of Churches and the Orthodox Churches.[4]

Christian mission has to consider the socio-cultural context. A core element of many cultures is harmony and interdependence. This is further compounded by the plurality of religions in the midst of which Christians are called to render their service. The Lord of the church reminds Christians how they are to be one so that the world may believe in them (Jn 17:21). The vexing problems that churches face with regard to ecumenism must be relativized in terms of the missionary priority. This missionary priority makes inter denominational confrontation obsolete and insignificant. The common Christian call to mission compels Christians to make use of ecumenical opportunities to be faithful to the Christian call to witness to the gospel. While the past cannot be changed, what the churches remember and celebrate today can affect Christian mission vitally.

No wonder, on the occasion of the commemoration of the 500 years of the Reformation the Lutheran World Federation and the Catholic church have taken further steps towards reconciliation and move forward in the field of joint service to express and strengthen their commitment to seek unity. This is amply expressed in their joint study document, "From Conflict to Communion."[5] It advocates how Catholics and Lutherans should witness together to the mercy of God in proclamation and service to the world. No 243 of the document reads: "Ecumenical engagement for the unity of the Church, does not serve only the Church, but also the world, so that the world may believe."

The disciples of Jesus, both the Catholics and the Lutherans, have the irreplaceable duty to be best advocates of human lives, animated by the Christian faith, in a secularised world. Christians believe that the God who sent Jesus Christ is working through his church, the community of his disciples, to confront evil and rebuild lives. In this spirit the two churches are looking forward to work together in harmony and collaboration.

The joint commission of Catholics and Lutherans pointed out in its statement in 1983, on the occasion of the 500th anniversary of Martin Luther's birth, that Christians, whether Protestants or Catholics, cannot disregard the person and message of this man.[6]"Luther's reforming agenda poses a spiritual and theological challenge for both contemporary Catholics and Lutherans."[7] They offer us both opportunities and obligations. This paper will emphasise the implications of Luther's teachings for the mission of the church especially with regard to the laity.

The 2017 quincentennial of the Reformation has added significance due to the fact that it is the first ecumenical celebration of the Reformation in which Catholics also participated. Equally, it offered Catholics the opportunity to interpret their theological tradition and mission adopting and accepting Luther's influence.

It is to be acknowledged that even if initially Catholics firewalled themselves against Luther's ideas, in the long run they had their impact on the Catholic Church as well. A major area of this impact was scripture. With his encyclical *Divino Aflante Spiritu,* the encyclical on the study of the scripture, Pope Pius XII opened the floodgates of the study of the scripture in the Catholic Church.

The joint declaration, From Conflict to Communion, underlined that the Reformation should be freed from the notion of separation or division in the church. What Luther intended was reform, not division which was the result of various factors, including the institutional failure to assess the situation. Equally, it was due to the political climate of the Supreme authority of the Holy Roman Empire from which many wanted to free themselves. Nor was it a 'rediscovery of the gospel' as many of the followers of Luther traditionally claimed.[8]

Even if the present cannot cancel what has happened in history, the remembrance can enable Christians to recreate the past for the present. They can narrate that history in a fresh way. The many secular events like the Universal Declaration of Human Rights by the United Nations (1948), the growing phenomenon of secularization, the revival of world's religions as well as the mutual influence of Catholics and Protestants, more so in recent times, all invite Christians to a new era of collaboration and unity. They impel Christians to search for what is common among them rather than what is dividing them and pursue ways of working towards overcoming the differences.

Centrality of Scripture

Until John Guttenberg's (1394-1468) discovery of the printing press, the Bible remained for ordinary Christians, by and large, a closed book, except for the occasional sermons and through art works. True, as pointed out earlier, there were trail-blazing minds such as that of John Wycliff and Jan Hus that attempted to popularize the Bible by translating it into local languages but they were met with stiff opposition. However, it is Luther's merit that he made scripture the integral part of Christian life.

Luther along with colleagues from the University of Wittenberg translated the New Testament into German and with the help of the recently introduced printing press made it easily accessible to ordinary Christians. Luther was a biblical scholar and was convinced of the power of the word of God in his own life.[9]

Luther recommended for the study of the scripture a process of three steps: prayer, meditation and affliction. One should read the scripture in the presence of God, in prayer and while meditating on the words of the scripture one must be attentive to the situations in life that often seem to contradict what is found in the scripture. Through this process the scripture proves its authority by overcoming those afflictions. "Note that the struggle of the Scripture is this, that it is not changed into the one who studies it, but that it transforms one who loves it into itself and its strength."[10] A person not only interprets the scripture but is also interpreted by it, which is the power and authority of the scripture.

Luther's central teaching that the Bible is the core source of religion and authority opened a rising wave of interest in the study of the scripture and this has continued to the present.

The Common Priesthood

An associate idea of Luther, and flowing from the centrality of the scripture, is the dignity and responsibility of every baptized person. In contrast to the prevailing medieval division of

Christians into spiritual (hierarchy) and temporal (the laity), Luther insisted how all Christians are priests in the eyes of God and that they have direct access to God. In his letter to the German nobility he put forward the doctrine that all baptized Christians were priests and spiritual, dismissing the existence of two classes of believers, the spiritual and the secular.[11]

Luther understood the relationship of believers to Christ as a "joyful exchange, in which the believer takes part in the properties of Christ, and thus also in his priesthood."[12] Commenting on 1 Peter 2:9, "You are a chosen race, a royal priesthood, a holy nation, God's own people," Luther insisted, "We are all consecrated priests through baptism."[13] Similarly, in his writing, *On the Babylonian Captivity of the Church* (1520) he wrote: "In this way we are all priests, as many of us are Christians. There are indeed priests whom we call ministers."[14]Luther held that all Christians are truly of the spiritual estate, and there are no differences among them, except that of office.[15] "There is no true basic difference between layman and priests, princes and bishops, between religious and secular, except for the sake of office and work, but not for the sake of authority."[16] Commenting on 1 Corinthians 12:12, "For just as the body is one and has many members, and all the members of the body, though many, are one body, so it is with Christ," he explained, "This applies to all of us because we have one baptism, one gospel, one faith, and are all equally Christians. For baptism, gospel and faith alone make men (sic) religious and create a Christian people."[17]

However, Luther's teaching on the Common Priesthood of the baptized was not at the expense of the ministerial priesthood. In article 14 of his *Augsburg Confession,* he wrote: "No one should publicly teach or administer sacraments in the church unless properly called."[18] It may also be pointed out how all through his career at the University of Wittenberg there used to be ordinations for the ministerial priests.

Even if Luther made a distinction between priesthood and ministers who have an office in the church as a preacher, the fact of sharing in Christ's priesthood is an invitation to share in Christ's ministry, to witness to the gospel that Christ did all through his ministry. This is significant for the mission of the church today which the chapter will develop in the following pages.

Vatican II and Luther

As the Catholic-Lutheran joint document, From Conflict to Communion, points out, today Catholics and Lutherans are able to narrate the story of Luther and his reformation together, overcoming traditional mutual prejudices that, in the past, frequently afflicted the interpretation of each other (no 35). In fact, some of the fresh teachings of the Second Vatican Council have their remote incubation beginning with Luther.

A major aspect of Luther's call for reform was his invoking the importance of the Bible and its role in Christian life. The Bible is so fundamental to Vatican II that most of its teachings are founded on the Bible, in contrast to the earlier Councils. Already in 1943 Pope Pius XII, through his encyclical *Divino Afflante Spiritu,* had liberated Catholic biblical research that had suffered a setback due to the fear of 'modernism,' and encouraged Catholic scholars to use critical methods in the study of scripture and this in turn paved the way for one of the key texts of Vatican II, *Dei Verbum,* the Dogmatic Constitution on Divine Revelation.

The very opening sentence of *Dei Verbum* signals the biblical spirit that envelops the Council as well as this document specifically: "Hearing the Word of God reverently and proclaiming it confidently..." (DV 1). The Bible is the narrative of salvation history in terms of the words and deeds of God, intrinsically bound together (DV 2). *Dei Verbum* made the word of God central to the life and worship and spirituality of the church and affirmed how the teaching authority of the church is not above the Word of God but stands at its service (DV 10). "The force and power in the Word of God is so great that it stands as the support and energy of the Church, the strength of faith for her sons, the food of the soul, the pure and everlasting source of spiritual life" (DV 21). Therefore, *Dei Verbum* admonishes the faithful to read Scripture through which God speaks to them (DV 25). It calls for a biblical revival in the formation of priests, in liturgy, in the church's mission and in every aspect of the church's life. In short, the document set in motion a biblical culture that underpinned the huge renewal program that the Council gave rise to.

Vatican II was a reforming Council and the greatest impact of this was felt in the very self-perception of the church as "a sacrament of God's reign in the world" (LG 8). Its identity is to serve as a sign to the world, its vocation is to actualize and to symbolize God's reign in its life and through this inviting the world to be transformed to this divine reign and this is done by the church as a whole. In contrast to the previously held view of perceiving the hierarchy as the main part of the church, Vatican II defined the church as "the people of God" (LG 10) with different ministries. This is an acknowledgement of the significance of every member of the church. No wonder, in the decree on the religious life, the Council spoke of the "Universal Call to Holiness," in sharp contrast to different states of perfection!

The church as a sign, with the same call to holiness of all members, reminds all Christians how they all share in the same mission of bringing the message of the good news of God's reign to the world. *Lumen Gentium,* the Dogmatic Constitution on the church, rather than beginning with the Pope and the hierarchy and working downwards, in the first two chapters describes the church as a mystery and as the people of God. The following chapters speak about the hierarchy, situating it as a service to the people of God. Further, *Lumen Gentium* (and later the Mission Decree *Ad Gentes* as well) showed how the church, as the continuation of God's reaching out to the world through Jesus Christ and God's Spirit, is missionary by its very nature. To be involved in mission is the very purpose of its existence.

The Council, thus, was a liberating and, hence, an exuberant event in the life of the church, of the Catholic Community. The fresh starting point is the perspective on mission, as projecting the image of the Kingdom, always inviting the world to be conformed to the Kingdom. Equally significant is the description of the church as a community, sharing in the priesthood of Christ, making every Christian responsible to witness to the Good News. The Council's teachings "make a serious claim on the conscience of the Catholic Christian," wrote the German theologian and Cardinal, Walter Kasper.[19]

In as much as the Council found it appropriate to enact a decree on the laity, *Apostolicam Actuositatem,* (AA) and lay concerns were treated in many Conciliar discourses, one can qualify the Council as a 'Council of the laity'.[20] The laity came a long way from the status: 'pay, obey and pray' or better in the words of Pope Pius X, "the one duty of the laity is to allow themselves to be led and, like a docile flock, to follow their pastors,"[21] to that of being called to assume their responsibility to be actively involved in the church's mission (LG 30, 33).

As the internationally recognized Canadian Canonist Ladislas Orsy pointed out, already in 1938 Pope Pius XI said, while addressing a group of seminarians in Rome: "The Church, the mystical body of Christ, has become a monstrosity. The head is very large but the body is shrunken. You the priests must rebuild that body of the Church and the only way in which you can rebuild it is to mobilize the lay people. You must call upon the lay people to become, along with you, the witnesses to Christ. You must call them especially to bring Christ back to the workplace, the market place."[22] The prophetic words of the Pope about rebuilding the church got underway with Vatican II by rectifying the disproportionality of the various parts of the body of the church. No doubt, the efforts of Catholic Religious Orders like the Dominicans, the Jesuits and others, as well as the writings of many theologians like Yves Congar, Joseph Cardign and others,[23] prepared the way for Vatican II in its retrieval of the role and dignity of the laity in the church.

Dolores R. Lecky wrote: "By the time the Second Vatican Council was convened in the fall of 1962, the movements and organizations that had been promoting increased responsibility for the laity within the Church and those that had been exploring the new frontiers of Christian education converged in significant ways."[24] For the first time the Council was attended also by laymen and women, even if only as 'auditors'. Similarly, qualified lay persons like Patrick Keegan, President of the Catholic Workers'

Movement, addressed the Council. No wonder the Decree on the Laity stated: "Since in our time women are taking increasingly active share in the whole life of the society, it is very important that their participation in the various sections of the Church's apostolate should likewise develop" (AA 9).

AA no 4 while situating family life within secular concerns and as a means of holiness in the life of the laity uses the idea of vocation. The very use of the word 'vocation' is significant in so far as it was a word used almost exclusively to refer to the call of priests and religious. The laity are called by God to forward the reign of God in the world and in the church (AA 4). The spirit of God is making the laity more conscious of their calling and their responsibility. The Council made it foundational that the laity share in the redemptive responsibility of the church, participating in the priestly, prophetic and royal office of Jesus Christ confirmed by the sacraments of Baptism and Confirmation (AA 2). There is a diversity of ministry in the church to fulfil the one mission (AA 2).

Laity and the Mission of the Church Today

Vatican II's affirmation of the vocation of the laity anchored on Baptism and Confirmation is very much scriptural. Already in the Old Testament, just before Israel is made as God's people through the covenant (Ex 20-24), God informs the people of the very purpose of the whole process: "That you may be holy and a priestly people, and a kingly nation..." (Ex 19:5-6). Israel is constituted as God's people for the sake of a mission, that they may serve as light to the nations (Is 42: 6, 49:6). The role of a priest and a king is that of service to the people.

Exodus 19:5-6 is almost verbatim repeated by St. Peter in his first letter to the Christian community: "You are a chosen race, a royal priesthood, a holy nation, God's own people that you may declare the wonderful deeds of him who call you out of darkness into his marvellous light" (1 Pt 2:9). The purpose of the Christian community is precisely that it may declare the wonderful deeds of God.

The missionary vocation of the Christian community is reflected in every page of the New Testament. Evangelist Mark is very precise in his call narrative: "He called unto him whom he was wanting to call and made them twelve – created a community - to be with him and to be sent out to proclaim and to cast out demons" (3:14-15).[25] Though there are individual differences among the evangelists the major elements are common to all: creation of a new community, presence of the community with the Lord and mission through word and deed. It is obvious from Acts 11:19ff that the risen Lord's mandate to be witnesses to him in Jerusalem and to the ends of the world (Acts 1:8) is discharged by the community as a whole. Interestingly, the very first Gentile community is the fruit, not of any of the Apostles' proclamation, but of the ordinary Christians (Acts 11:19-26).

However, the Post-Constantinean era witnessed a steady marginalization of the laity in the church, especially with regard to their role in mission. This was aggravated also due to the changed understanding of mission. If mission in the Apostolic era was primarily a matter of sharing of an experience leading to transformation (see 1Jn 1:1-4), to serve the world in the same way as the soul does to the body,[26] gradually it becomes a question of conquest, displacement and expansion, especially, during the colonial days. It was executed by professional missionaries belonging to the religious orders, who were sent to the 'pagan lands' to save the souls of 'the natives.' That missionary era began to change with Vatican II.

Luther rightly insisted on the beauty and dignity of Christian baptism. However, due to his polemic against the Roman Curia, he did not devote equal space to the duties that baptism brings to every Christian, more so the missionary character of baptism. It is to the merit of Vatican II that the Council spelt out the missionary nature of the whole church, basing it solidly on God as love. The greatest insight of Vatican II, I would suggest, is its declaration that God is a "fountain like love" (AG 2). The first five articles of the Mission Decree *Ad Gentes* spells out this love further in terms of God's reaching out to the world through God's Word Incarnate, Jesus Christ and through God's Spirit. As the nature of love is reaching out, the whole process of mission can be described as the divine dynamism of self-reaching out, beginning with creation. Obviously, this describes in the church's existence as mission in which all the baptized take part.

True, *Ad Gentes* used the traditional concept of sending. In so far as sending is more congenial to a geographical sense of mission, not to speak of its colonial hangovers, and since the contemporary context of mission is much more complex than geography or culture, mission has to make use of the self-diffusive nature of the divine love, as reaching out. This would be more meaningful when we speak of the mission of the laity in so far as they are not, normally, sent out as are the professional missionaries.

In Jesus Christ God entered human history and Jesus told his listeners how in him God's reign has come (Mk 1:15, Mt 4:17). Love and service are foundational to divine reign. When a lawyer asked Jesus, what was the basic norm of life, Jesus replied to him through the love command and outlined Christian life through the parable of the good Samaritan (Lk 10: 25-37). This is the good news of the gospel. Vatican II's reform movement was precisely to take this good news to the heart of every human person, in his/her living context.[27] Every Christian is called to bring this good news to the neighbour through the practice of the Christian reaching out to the neighbour.

Christian living cannot be limited to certain devotional practices or the Sunday masses, but must include a genuine Christian outlook that does not shutout the neighbour. Mary's concern for the wedding host who ran out of wine must inspire any Christian. Reaching out to anyone who is in genuine need is the ultimate Christian value (Lk 10:37). The Christian preoccupation is not so much the salvation of one's soul as much as becoming a blessing to others even as Abraham is called to be a blessing to all the families of the world (Gen 12:3). That is how, the common identity of the church as the light to the world (Mt 5:13-14), is concretized at the individual level. Only then can we appreciate the Lucan inaugural proclamation of the Lord (Lk 4:16-19).

The prophetic dimension of Christian baptism sharing in the mission of the prophet from Nazareth (Mt 21:11), must be exercised by every Christian. In a world where there is so much self-seeking and lying, the very Christian life has to become an unsettling presence, powerful enough to effect a disturbance in the hearts and minds of the onlookers. Such a missionary perspective is present in most documents of Vatican II but more so in the Pastoral Constitution of the church in the Modern World, *Gaudium et Spes*. Having said how the church, "coming forth from the eternal Father's love, founded in time by Christ the Redeemer and made one in the Holy Spirit," article 40 of *Gaudium et Spes* goes on to say: "she serves as a leaven and a kind of soul for the human society[28] as it is to be renewed in Christ and transformed into God's family."

All this spells out the baptismal foundation of mission rather than the priestly ordination or the religious vows, though the ordained ministers in their ministry can raise the awareness of the Christian community of its basic call to mission and to do everything possible that the community fulfils this vocation. Through their baptism Christians are 'reconfigured' (Gaillardetz) so as to have this constant habitual outlook of reaching out, even as the Good Samaritan did. The vocation of the laity for mission is not transitional or substitutional, i.e., temporary or filling a gap. It is the permanent call to make present God's other-centeredness experiential to people, and thus to become 'God with us, Emmanuel' (Mt 1:23).

This is a challenge for the Christian community that it refocuses its attention on the ministry of Jesus Christ than having an exaggerated concern for an other-worldly saviour or similar theological preoccupations.

Retrieve the Ministry of Jesus

Dominic Crossan begins his magisterial volume, *The Historical Jesus: the Life of a Mediterranean Jewish Peasant*, with the assertion, "In the beginning was the performance, not the word alone, not the deed alone, but both, each indelibly marked with the other forever."[29] Similarly, Geza Vermes, an authority in Jewish studies, in the introduction to his book, *Jesus the Jew*, points out how the church in formulating its profession of faith has a "passionate interest in Christ's eternal pre-existence and glorious after-life, but of his earthly career the faithful are told next to nothing, save that he was born and died."[30] Granted that

that situation is changing in the light of the scriptural research as well as the influence of liberation theology, there is still great need to return to the ministry of the Lord rather than focusing predominantly on the Paschal Mystery or similar doctrinal considerations. For, as Jose A. Pagola has spelt out, "We begin to encounter Jesus when we begin to trust God as he did, when we believe in love as he did, when we come to suffering people as he did, when we defend life as he did, when we look at people as he did, when we confront life and death with hope as he did, when we pass on the contagion of the Good News as he did."[31]

As a historical religion that bases its origin on the words and deeds of Jesus Christ, it is simply imperative that Christianity formulates its faith and mission in the light of the ministry of Jesus as the apostles did. Peter summarized the whole earthly life of Jesus in his very first address to a Gentile community by saying "he went about doing good" (Act 10:38). Similarly he refers to Jesus in his Pentecost witness by stating how Jesus was "a man attested to you by God with mighty works and wonders and signs which God did through him in your midst, as you yourselves know…" (Act 2:22).

The Christian mission is nothing more and nothing less than what Jesus did, i.e.: manifest God his father (Jn 1:18; 14:9) and usher in his reign (Mk 1:14; Mt 4:17; Lk 4:18-19). The core message of Jesus was the in-breaking of the divine reign, that was available to all those who cared to follow him.[32] John Shelby Spong has argued, what the gospels tell is "the presence of God in a contemporary moment, they interpreted this moment by applying to it similar moments in their sacred story when they were convinced the presence of God had also been real to their forebears in faith."[33] That was the only way they could understand and process the God presence they found in Jesus that was so powerful.[34] The gospels interpret the God-experience encountered in Jesus of Nazareth as the *good news* (Mk 1:1).

In the ministry of Jesus, we encounter "the conduit through which the love of God was loosed into human history."[35] In his ministry he became the expression of the very being of God. To have the courage to be himself, delivered from the need to please, to impress, to protect, to win, but to live authentically the self he was. The key question for Christians is not so much if Jesus was God, "but whether they believe that God is Jesus-like," comments George Maloney.[36] In Jesus God becomes a "God-toward-others by communicating Himself through His Word and His Spirit of love."[37]

Jesus is the Kingdom of God, and the theme of the Kingdom of God, occurring over fifty times, is the most characteristic and the most distinctive "feature of Jesus' preaching."[38] James Dunn writes: "More striking still, however, would have been Jesus' affirmation that the Kingdom had already come, or was already active in the present."[39]

As scriptural scholars like Tom Wright[40] have shown, at the time of Jesus one of the major challenges that Israel lived with was the Roman rule to which different groups responded differently. The Jewish leaders of the time, by and large, aligned with the Romans, while groups like the Essenes waited for God to act liberating them from the foreign rule, in contrast to the Zealots who had recourse to armed revolt. It is in this background that Jesus came with the message of the arrival of the divine reign.

Jesus was not an abstract teacher of philosophical truths but acted as a prophet who explained the meaning of the kingdom that had been inaugurated in and through him. It was radically different from any of the prevailing notions and attitudes. Rather than finding refuge in isolation, he mingled with tax collectors and sinners. Instead of armed rebellion he took the path of peace, and forgiveness, turning the other cheek when struck, without abandoning justice (Jn 19:23).

As he taught his disciples to pray for the arrival of the divine reign already now, his constant mission was the ringing in of this reign through his deeds of healing, feeding, casting out demons, forgiving, giving new lease of life as well as through his teaching. He made the kingdom visibly present through his all-inclusive table-fellowships, which we come across frequently in the gospels. "Jesus", as Michael McCabe, writes, "was not just pointing to the Kingdom of God, but was in his words, deeds and person actually embodying God's kingly rule."[41] Jesus showed how he would win the messianic victory over evil and build the true temple through his ministry leading to the cross and resurrection. This prompted the Jewish scholar Ed Kessler to write: "For Jews, the significance of Jesus must be in his life rather than his death; in his teaching rather than in doctrine; in the holiness of his life rather than in the sanctity of belief."[42]

The Greco-Roman inculturation that began already with the Nicene Creed shifted the biblical realism on the understanding of Jesus as God's presence ushering in the reign of God, to an abstract intellectualistic Christology. This reached its height during the colonial period that went unchallenged due to the presumed cultural and social superiority of the Christian West. In the post-colonial period few are prepared to buy the claims of superiority or exclusivism. This, in turn, is an invitation to return to the gospel realism that has its emphasis on the ministry of the Lord who went about doing good. Today, as

Dominic Crossan has drawn our attention to, a sapiential vision is needed "for discerning how, here and now in this world, one can so live that God's power, rule, and dominion are evidently present to all observers."[43]

The Kingdom that we encounter in the ministry of Jesus is not primarily an eschatological one to come about at the end of times, "nor did it refer to a geographical area or a political entity but to a set of relationships that actually obtain or should obtain, between creator and creatures, between God and the world."[44] The ministry of Jesus shows how the old age is crumbling and a new one is emerging right now. This is the meaning of the parables and the miracles of Jesus as narrated in the gospels. In contrast to the classical expositions of the doctrine of the person and expiatory work of Christ neglecting the earthly ministry of Jesus, we come across works like that of Leonhard Goppelt that portray the importance of Jesus' ministry for the church.[45] Scripture scholar and theologian Sean Freyne underlines in his influential article, "The Galilean Jesus and a Contemporary Christology," that only a historico-theological approach can "illustrate the universal meaning that is disclosed in and through the particularity of Jesus' life. God did not become human as a universal, but in the particularity of the life and praxis of Jesus."[46] Obviously, this particularity is revealed through his incarnation and ministry.

The life of Jesus, with the emphasis on what he said and did, is the guiding principle for the church in so far as its basic vocation is to follow the Lord. Scripture scholars can shed ever new light on that life for each age to follow the Lord in his ministry so that the church becomes the light to the world (Mt 5:13-14). Though the church never advocated an exclusive Easter-Jesus, gnostic writings indeed caused to minimize the importance of the pre-Easter Jesus, with less reference to the historical Jesus. The evangelists, however, focus their readers' attention on the Jesus who began his ministry by announcing the arrival of the eschatological Kingly rule of God, with the "fulfilment of time" (Mk 1.15).

A follower of Jesus cannot remain encased in his/her own world with little concern for the world outside, for discipleship is a call to be inserted into the very ministry of Jesus by following the same path (*halakha*) and thus to become a light to the world (Mt 5:13-14). Referring to Jesus' practice of love, N.T. Wright comments: "Jesus shares the pollution of sickness and death, by the power of his own love – and it is a love, above all, that shines through these stories – turns that pollution into wholeness and hope."[47] Through his ministry Jesus becomes a divine manifestation, epiphany, and simultaneously, the manifestation of the humans, anthropophany.

Following the Lord can be only through following his ministry that brings one to the joy of the banqueting Lord (Mk 2:18-19), banqueting with the outcasts, compassionate association with the marginalized, and thus preaching the good news to the poor. Through that kind of mission Christians come face to face with Jesus, the epiphany of God.[48] Through such a practice Christians anticipate the end-times already now. To quote Tom Wright, "Perhaps they are the sort of things that might just be characteristic of the *new creation,* of the fulfilled time, of what happens when heaven and earth come together."[49] By way of conclusion, the cleansing of the temple (Jn 2:14-17 and the Synoptic Par) capsules what has been said: Jesus' ministry that led him to the cross and resurrection, was a self-giving, out of "zeal for God's house" (Jn 2: 17; Ps 69:1), God's reign, "the divine house-hold"[50]. As Pope Benedict XVI has shown evangelist

Matthew concludes the account of the cleansing of the temple by observing: "The blind and the lame came to him in the temple and he healed them" (21:14).[51] The purified temple, the community of his disciples, is to serve the cause of healing and wholeness of life, more so for those driven to the margins of life and society. Following the Lord can be only through following his ministry that brings one to the joy of the banqueting Lord (Mark 2:18-19), banqueting with the outcasts, compassionate association with the marginalized, and thus preaching the good news to the poor. Through that kind of mission Christians come face to face with Jesus, the epiphany of God.[52]

Endnotes

[1] Hans Kung, *Christianity: The Religious Situation of Our Time,* (London: Collins, 1995, 525). The humanistic revival that began during the late middle ages, to a large extent, paved the way for the reformation. People wanted to hear more enlightened sermons from the ministers. (See John Dillenberger, *Martin Luther, Selections from his Writings* (Garden City, NY: Anchor Books, 1961, 166). Similarly, John Wycliffe (1320-1384), a century before Luther, had advocated the translation of the Bible into English and it influenced Jan Hus (1352-1445) who, though, was burned at the stake.

[2] Luther, in his struggle, sought the help of the Nobility of Germany, as he felt powerless before the well-entrenched institutional power of the church of the time. Luther was convinced of the need for a General Council to discuss and usher in reform, especially with regard to the spiritual authority that the church claimed to have, namely, to change divine will regarding a person who is in purgatory to be taken out by a substitutionary order of the church in the form of a total indulgence which one could win for oneself or for one in purgatory, by paying money for the construction of the basilica of St. Peter.

[3] https://w2.vatican.va/content/francesco/en/speeches/2016/october/documents/papa-francesco_20161031_svezia-evento-ecumenico.html (accessed on 20/01/2017).

[4] See the Declaration on Ecumenism (*Unitatis Redentigratio*) of Vatican II. The Church: Towards a Common Vision, Faith and Order Paper 214, WCC.

[5] From Conflict to Communion. Lutheran-Catholic Common Commemoration of the Reformation in 2017. www.bonifatius.de.

[6] From Conflict to Communion, no 2.

[7] From Conflict to Communion, no 3.

[8] As mentioned in foot note 1, persons like John Wycliffe and Jan Hus had already advocated the need for translating the Bible into the languages of the people and the place of the Bible in the lives of the faithful.

[9] Cf. Ronald D. Witterup, *Rediscovering Vatican II: Scripture* (New York: Paulist Press, 2006), 5.

[10] Luther, *First Lecture on the Psalms,* in Herbert J.A. Bouman, *Luther's Writings, WA 3,* 397, 9-11, quoted in Conflict and Communion, no.197.

[11] See *An Appeal to the Ruling Class,* in *Reformation Writings of Martin Luther,* Bertran Lees Woolf (ed.), Library of Ecclesiastical History, 1952, 114.

[12] See From Conflict to Communion, no 162.

[13] Letter to the Christian Nobility, in *Weinmar Gusgabe* 6, p.407. See Conflict and Communion, foot note no 3.

[14] Ibid. I may add that this idea is foreshadowed already in the Old Testament when God reminds the people just before the making of the Covenant that they are to be a holy, priestly and kingly people at the service of God (Ex 19: 5-6).

[15] See Helmut T Lehmann (ed.), *Luther's Works* (Philadelphia, PA: Fortress Press, 1970), 5.

[16] Lehmann, 14.

[17] Bertran Lees Woolf (ed.), "An Appeal to the Ruling Class," in *Reformation Writings of Martin Luther,* 113.

[18] Timothy J Wengert, *Priesthood, Pastors, Bishops: Public Ministry for the Reformation and Today,* (Minneapolis: Fortress Press, 2008), v.

[19] Walter Kasper, *Theology and Church* (London: SCM Press, 1989), 9.

[20] Dolores R. Lecky, *The Laity and Christian Education* (New York: Paulist Press, 2006), 1.

[21] Ibid.

[22] Ladislas Orsy, *Receiving the Council* (Collegeville: Liturgical Press, 2009), 36, quoted by Neil Ormerod, "The Laity in the Australian Church," in N. Ormerod *et al.*(eds), *Vatican II: Reception and Implementation in the Australian Church* (Mulgrave, Vic: Garratt Pub., 2012), 62.

[23] The late Cardinal Valerian Gracias of Bombay made a presentation at the World Congress for the Lay Apostolate in 1951 advocating a theology of the laity who shared responsibility for the church's mission. Others like Cardinal Newman, Cardinal Suhard, G.K. Chesterton, Frank Sheed, Maisie Ward *et al.*, had their formative impact on the Council.

[24] Dolores Lecky, *The Laity and Christian Education,* 11.

[25] This is my translation of the original Greek text.

[26] Cf. *Letter to Diognetus*, 6.

[27] The Pastoral Constitution of the church, *Gaudium et Spes,* which deals with this service to the world, begins with the words: "The joys, the agonies and the aspirations of the world are our joys, our agonies and our aspirations..." (GS 1).

[28] *Letter to Diognetus,* an early church document, taught how Christians were to serve the world as soul did to the body (n 6).

[29] Dominic J. Crossan, *The Historical Jesus: The Life of a Mediterranean Jewish Peasant* (New York: HarperCollins, 1991), XI.

[30] Geza Vermes, *Jesus the Jew* (New York: Macmillan Pub.co,1973), 15.

[31] Jose A. Pagola, *Jesus: An Historical Approximation* (Miami, Fl: 2012), 28.

[32] Steve Chalke & Alan Mann, *The Lost Message of Jesus* (Grand Rapids, MI: Zondervan, 2003), 16.

[33] John Shelby Spong, *Liberating the Gospels: Reading the Bible with Jewish Eyes* (New York: HarperCollins, 1996), 19.

[34] Ibid 20.

[35] Ibid 332.

[36] George A. Maloney, *Bright Darkness: Jesus the Lover of Mankind* (Denville, JJ: Dimension Books, 1977), 6.

[37] Ibid, 11.

[38] James D.G. Dunn, *Who was Jesus* (London: SPCK, 2016), 16.

[39] Ibid, 17.

[40] Tom Wright, *The Challenge of Jesus,* (London: SPCK, 2000).

[41] Michael McCabe, "New Perspectives on the Historical Jesus and His Mission," *Sedos Bulletin,* 41(March-April 2009): 52.

[42] Ed Kessler, *Jesus,* Gloucestershire (UK: The History Press, 2016), 92.

[43] Dominic Crossan, *Jesus A Revolutionary Biography,* 56.

[44] Robert W. Funk, *Honest to Jesus: Jesus for a New Millennium* (Rydalmere, NSW: Hodder & Stoughton Book, 1996), 166.

[45] Leonhard Goppelt, *Theology of the New Testament: The Ministry of Jesus in its Theological Significance* (Grand Rapids, MI: Eerdmans Pub. Co., Vol 1, 1981 & Vol 2, 1982).

[46] Sean Freyne, "The Galilean Jesus and a Contemporary Christology," *Theological Studies,* Vol 70/2, June 2009: 281, 281-297.

[47] N.T. Wright, *Luke for Everyone,* (Louiseville: John Knox Press, 2004), 105.

[48] Marcus Borg, *Jesus: A New Vision,* (New York: HarperCollins, 1991), 191.

[49] Tom Wright, *Simply Jesus (London*: SPCK, 2011), 133.

[50] John Dominic Crossan, *The Greatest Prayer (New* York: HarperCollins, 2010), 3.

[51] Pope Benedict XVI, *Jesus of Nazareth (*San Francisco: Ignatius Press, 2011), 23.

[52] Borg, M. *Jesus: A New Vision* (New York: HarperCollins, 1991), 191.

Chapter - 8

Role of the Family in Christian Mission

As part of its process of *ressourcement,* Vatican II retrieved the role and significance of marriage and family in the church.[1] In fact the Council presented the church as a family of God along with suggestions that it should become a family centred on ministry.[2] In most cultures, family is the basic social unit that serves as the school for inculcating the primary lessons of socialization as well as social values that are dear to the society. This chapter will discuss the significance of family in human cultures, more so in Asian culture, and will discuss the role of the family in mission and the pastoral service fostering that service by the church, rendering the family as a key unit of Christian mission for contemporary society.

Religious Background of Family

From time immemorial, family served as the seminal ground for transmitting religious thoughts and religious teachings. In fact, it is in the intimacy of the family that most religions have their origin. The foundational Hindu scriptures, the Vedas and the Upanishads, have their origin in the family in so far as these were composed from the oral tradition that was transmitted from father to son, sitting close-by (*upa-ni-sad*).

Rigveda, the root of primary revelation, *Sruti,* in Hinduism, is a collection of family rituals that were practised for millennia. Well-known scholar of Vedic texts, Frits Staal, points out how language and rituals were transmitted from father to son. "Fathers insisted that sons learned Vedic text until transmission became ritualized."[3]

Buddhism, a religion of much later origin and which began as a reform movement within Hinduism, also had its association with the family tradition, especially that of Mahakasyapa who codified the oral texts after Buddha.[4] However, it has to be mentioned that in Buddhism, especially in the Theravada Tradition, marriage is stripped of all its spiritual enchantment, in so far as Buddhism demands a very high degree of renunciation for liberation (Nirvana) to which "marriage is never a salvific experience according to the orthodox tradition, in so far as celibacy is a condition for ultimate human emancipation."[5] However, even in Buddhism, following the general dharma, way, marriage is part of the moral persuasion, rather than legal enforcement.[6]

Chinese religions, under the impact of Confucius, laid stress on family relations. Parents are to be kind to children who in turn must honour parents. Older children must set an example to the younger ones. "When brothers live in concord and at peace, the strain of harmony shall never cease."[7] Confucian teachings have upheld the values of filial piety and care of the elderly as part of the communitarian culture.

Christianity too has had an influence on the making of the family system in so far as Christianity has an Asian origin and existed in parts of Asia from apostolic times. With its theology of creation, prophetic service and the kingdom vision proclaimed by Jesus, Christianity contributes to the religious vision of family.

The roots of an Asian family system are to be found among the indigenous peoples of Asia who in addition to the total acceptance of children as divine gift and the future of the family, based family on the relationship to the land from the primordial times, *in illo tempore*.[8]

Sacredness of the Family

In the words of late Pope John Paul II, "The family – based on marriage between a man and a woman – is the first and fundamental unit of society and is a sanctuary of creation and nurturing of children."[9]Traditional Asian family is built on the sacredness of the marriage between a man and a woman and it is considered to be the norm.[10] It is a *sanskara*, sacrament and it initiates a family. According to the Ngaju Dayak of South Borneo marriage is connected with the conception of God and creation. It is not simply a social occasion, but one of the most important religious affairs. "To be married means to enter a new stage of sacred life."[11]

Generally speaking what characterizes Asian family is the joy flowing from love and communion, between parents, siblings and grand-parents. This in turn serves also as a support system to preserve the religious and social values of Asian society. Family is the close-knit unit of society sustaining lasting relationship and enduring solidarity despite all sorts of peer pressures.[12] Frequently through marriage not only are two individuals united into a new family, but also the two respective families and the near relations are united into a greater, wider "family," extending love, concern, respect and similar values.

As the Federation of Asian Bishops' Conferences, in its eighth Plenary Assembly affirmed, there prevails in Asian families a culture of life.[13] The Bishops based their reflections on Asian Family on "the hope, the aspiration, the dream of the Asian family for life in its fullness."[14] Even in the face of untold misery and poverty, Asian families maintain this hope.

An important dimension of that respect for life is that, despite the many social tremors such as the neo-liberal trends justifying divorce and similar vicissitudes against family life, Asia continues to hold marriage as sacred and as the source of children. Children are considered to be a divine gift and parents take pleasure and joy for the sacrifices they undertake for their children and ensure that they provide the best healthcare and education that they can afford for their children.

The close-knit nature of the family is proverbial. Parents and grandparents, as well as the sick members of the family are special objects of love and care. The elders still command respect and their counsel and example maintain family unity. The intimate family system provides the right atmosphere for absorbing not only human values but also religious values. Family thus becomes the cradle for fostering a sense of the divine as well as for inculcating the primary religious lessons.[15] The religiosity of the family is nurtured through the many religious observances such as family prayers, listening to the religious scriptures and religious celebrations.

Family bonds and traditions preserve the resilience of the Asian family even in the face of setbacks and economic challenges. Asian families continue to serve as the nursery for

Kingdom values like love, sharing, equality, respect, hospitality, forgiveness and others. These along with the religiosity of the family keep the family bond stable as a house built on solid foundation (Mt 7:24-25). Asian family, thus, is a sort of the sacrament of the reign of God.

Family, in general, could be described as the primary medium of religious experience, the fertile ground for the religious seed to sprout and take root. Family opens the primary channels of God-experience and to respond to the demands and challenges of day to day life, firmly anchoring the roots of commitment to the Transcendent, at the same time bestowing a personal engagement with the Transcendent. In Asia where religion is a "spiritual force" family becomes the space for spiritual realization.[16]

Dark side of Asian Family

Admittedly, Asian family has contributed also to the practice of patriarchy and the maintenance of the caste system in the case of India. The mother of the family frequently had only a secondary role in decision making. Frits Staal invites our attention to the fact that the Vedas hardly ever mention the mother.[17] There was a pattern of dependence of women on men, even if there were matriarchal and matrilineal tribes and clans in India and elsewhere in Asia. As far as India is concerned, though the Vedas do not mention the secondary role of women, a much later text, the Code of *Manusmrti,* of second century CE origin, imposed the norm, "as a child a girl must remain under her father's control, as a woman, under her husband, and when her husband is dead, under her son."[18]

Undeniably, patriarchy remains the determining factor in Asian families even as in Asian societies. To quote the Asian

Bishops, "The worldview of patriarchy lies deep in the cultural and religious subconscious of Asia and dominates politics, economics, human relationships, community roles, etc."[19] It leads to the male exercise of power in the family, at the same time reducing women to meekness, submission and subordination, tolerating infidelities of men and their irresponsible behaviour while strict behavioural demands are imposed on women. Male domination can and does contribute to social evils like preference for the male child and pre-natal sex determination tests, often leading to abortion of baby girls.

Gender inequality in Asian societies begins in the families already where men enjoy a superior role. Authority and domination are unconsciously absorbed by men leading to paternal authoritarianism in family, relegating to women roles of submission and subordination.

Caste-consideration is integral to marriage, more so for arranged marriages and it is the prevalent form of marriages in India. This, in turn, has contributed to make caste an unbootable vice in Indian society, not excluding the church even if it is unchristian and has given rise to much violence, especially in the context of ministries and appointments. Exaggerated attention paid to caste divisions at the time of marriage keeps society fractured, obliterating the basic equality of human beings.

New Challenges

The Indian theologians in the declaration after their annual meeting at Kottayam, Kerala, 30 April – 3 May 2015 reflect the changed situation of the Asian family calling for matching changes in church's pastoral practice. "We express our conviction that the whole church in (India) needs to revisit the current theology of marriage and family and create a new praxis of pastoral care in the light of a liberative reading of the Word of God, the signs of the times and in the context of the Synod of Bishops on Family."[20] What the Indian theologians speak of India is to a large extent applicable to Asia in general.

"Asian family is a microcosm of Asian reality," declared the Asian Bishops.[21] Assailed from all sides by anti-family forces of dehumanization and disintegration, ranging from material poverty to secularization, values and external pressures are taking their toll on Asian family. Traditional families in Asia, as elsewhere, have come under the impact of globalization and mass media, bringing unprecedented changes.

A leading reality of the times as far as Asia is concerned is the large scale migration in the wake of globalization and the lure of better living conditions elsewhere. This has left both positive and negative impact on Asian families. The first and the most alarmingly damaging element is the separation of families, making either the husband or the wife work elsewhere, leaving the rest of the family in a spirit of perpetual separation. Apart from the forced separation of Asian families, this has caused the invasion of the sacred Asian family space by an avalanche of forces such neo-liberal culture of individualism, selfishness, life-styles and mind-sets motivated by consumeristic values. We have to bear in mind how the family is at the centre of the social turmoil affecting Asian society.

Instances of families with single parents, separated parents, or remarried parents are not any more, rare in Asia. The impact western culture brought in either through channels of communication or through migrant workers is shaping a new culture of anonymity and lack of concern for others. Inter- connectedness and interdependence are giving way to anonymity and disinterestedness. Marriages are becoming more fragile weakening marital and family bonds of intimacy and love. "Many no longer see marriage as a lifetime commitment," declared the Asian Bishops.[22] Under the impact of neo-liberal thinking and the spread of deviant ideologies the sacredness and the permanency of marriage are becoming suspect. Though rare, we come across couples who do not subscribe to the sacramentality of marriage but view it just a legal contract and would be satisfied by a civil marriage.

Another increasing experience is that of inter-cultural and inter-religious marriages along with the implied questions of mutual adjustment with regard to the practice of faith, especially the bringing up of children in Christian faith. Along with this we come across also ever increasing number of divorces. There are also instances of same sex partners, causing great challenge to traditional Asian family.

A major challenge to Asian family is poverty. Probably this was the first challenge to Asian family in some parts of Asia like the Philippines where mothers were forced to take up work as house maids in other parts of the world even much before the onslaught of globalization. Affected by poverty, due to unemployment or underemployment, many Asians are compelled to look for work elsewhere forcing them to live outside the protective family tradition.

Similarly, the recognition of the equality and dignity of men and women, along with the enhanced educational opportunities and economic pressures, have prompted women to take up work outside home, contributing not only to the financial power of the family but in decision making as well, even if this has not done away with wife-battering and other forms of discrimination and oppression against women at home and at work.

The emergence of new situations of migration, separation, wars and conflicts creates new challenges to the value of family life and meaning of human life demanding fresh understanding of Christian life and family. Traditional arranged marriages give way to inter-cultural and inter-religious marriages which though not bad in themselves can affect traditional family values.

In the name of progress or to be modern many try to replace traditional family values. As the FABC Theological Commission has pointed out: "Family relationships are weakened by the replacement of human communications by mass media. Traditional form of respect, reverence and relationships between elders and youngsters, between teachers and students, between leaders and people are reduced to the minimum. This is further aggravated by the separation of children from their parents who for economic reason are forced to be migrant workers."[23] This situation is compounded by the rising violence and fundamentalism fanned by vested interests destroying the very fabric of Asian culture, harmony.

Family Origin of Asian Church

The church in Asia had its origin centred on certain families even as the other New Testament churches (Act 2: 46).[24] According to the St. Thomas Christian tradition the Apostle Thomas converted certain families in India and ordained priests to lead the community. Thus, the priest Thomas Ramban Maliekel, the 48th priest of the Ramban family re-wrote the Ramban Song, an important historical document of the St. Thomas Christians, in the fifteenth century.[25] Cardinal Varkey Vithayathil points out how "some familes in Kerala like Kali, Kaiankave, Maliekal, etc., even today trace their origin to some Namboothiri families supposed to have been converted by St. Thomas."[26] This is corroborated also by Cardinal Eugene Tisserant, relying on the writings of ancient church historian, Eusebius, who refers to the Alexandrine Pantaenus finding Christians in India reading Mathew's gospel at the end of the second century C.E.[27]

Missionary Role of the Family

The church, constituted as the continuation of that divine self-reaching out in Jesus Christ through the Holy Spirit, is mission (AG 1-5). All that the church does, has to be an expression of that divine self-reaching out. The church is a community of "missionary disciples" (EG 120), "whose pastoral ministry in a missionary style is not obsessed with the disjointed transmission of a multitude of doctrines to be insistently imposed" (EG 35), but a constant reaching out to others seeking their good (EG 9) "to give life to others" (EG 10). Christian family is the fruit and future of this reaching out and life-giving process.

Christian approach to family must be based on the sound principle that marriage and family life are not inferior to celibate life. Rather, marriage is to be presented as the way of life in God's plan (Gen 1: 27-28) and celibacy has room only in the context of church's service to the kingdom (Mt 19:12). The word incarnate, Jesus of Nazareth had to grow up in a family, "he went down with them and came to Nazareth and was obedient to them" (Lk 2:51).

Jesus of Nazareth was not only nurtured in a family, but his ministry was a process of strengthening families through his word and deeds such as, healing (Mk 1:30-31), raising the dead (Lk 8:49-56), forgiving sins (Mk 5:22-24) and even saving a family from embarrassment (Jn 2:1-10). The root of family is love and Jesus made it foundational to discipleship (Jn 13:34).

The Roman Synod on family as well as the post-synodal Apostolic Exhortation, *Amoris Laetitiae,* (the joy of love), underlined the centrality of Christian family in mission by stating that with its life of joy and as the domestic church, it witnessed to the gospel (AL 200). Vatican II had already spelt out how the family, established by divine plan revealed in the creation of humans as male and female, with the mandate that man must leave his father and his mother and cleave to his wife, and that they become one flesh (Gen 2:24), is the symbol of the relation between Christ and the church (CL 11). The family is the basic and vital cell of Christian life and fulfil its mission as the domestic ecclesial community.

Built on the sacrament of marriage, Christian family reflects the divine love and communion. Hence John Paul II admonished Christian families saying: "The family has the mission to guard, reveal and communicate love" (FC 17). It becomes the living icon of God's own communion in the world. The kingdom as the divine household is a matter of communion.

Similarly, Pope Francis invites Christian families "to value the gifts of marriage and family, and to persevere in a love strengthened by the virtues of generosity, commitment, fidelity and patience" (AL 5). In the face of the challenges of modern life in the family such as the effects of both parents working and returning home exhausted, addiction to the mass media and social media, social conformism to gender discrimination, alcoholism, individualism, exclusion, violence, self-seeking and lack of communication, families have to go through a process of missionary conversion to become fertile ground for the full flowering of the baptismal call to shine as light to the world.

Integral to the en-fleshment of this mission, pastoral care to family has to help the family to become a nursery of values that will sustain the family against the vicissitudes that we have outlined earlier. It has to become a community of love that is ever ready to reach out to others in help with a spirit of hospitality and care. Family as the domestic church has to be helped to become a sacrament of the divine reign.

Asian family has to become a school that trains disciples of equals where boys and girls receive not only equal love and care but also equal opportunities and encouragement. This implies also the equality of the parents themselves without any gender discrimination or patriarchal domination.

A leading aspect of the pastoral care for the family in Asia will be the attention paid to inter-faith marriages. The couples in inter-faith marriages are to be supported by pastoral care that accompanies them with proper understanding of the symbols, rituals and festivals of the other religion that will enable them to take part in the sacred events of the partner with respect and devotion. The Catholic marriage partner has to be aware how that person remains fully part of the sacramental life of the church.[28]

Such a spirit permeates Pope Francis' concluding address to the Synod on the family, October 2015. The Pope emphasized how the aim of the Synod was "bringing the joy of hope without falling into a facile repetition of what is obvious or has already been said." He continued to bring home the purpose of the Synod as "trying to view and interpret realities, today's realities, through God's eyes, so as to kindle the flame of faith and enlighten people's hearts in times marked by discouragement, social, economic and moral crisis, and growing pessimism. It was about bearing witness to everyone that, for the church, the gospel continues to be a vital source of eternal newness, against all those who would "indoctrinate" it in dead stones to be hurled at others."[29] Overcoming the temptations to manipulation, exploitation, enslavement, violence and revenge, family offers that joy and hope that the Pope outlined. Through the life-long practice of self-giving, acceptance, forgiveness, solidarity and communication the family becomes an active agent of mission. Welcoming each other and new lives, the family extends the warm hospitality to neighbours and those in need.

Conclusion

Christian families are not left unaffected by post-modern culture. This in turn demands of them to face situations that are not always easy. The church has to accompany these families with pastoral involvement always motivated by the mission of love and compassion, always remaining a sacrament of the kingdom and enabling families to reflect the kingdom in their lives and witness to salvation in Jesus Christ. In spite of the shadows and weaknesses family remains the bedrock of Christian living. Vibrant Christian families hold the key to the renewal of the fabric of the whole ecclesial body, not to speak of the potential it holds to transform humanity as such.

Endnotes

[1] The Dogmatic Constitution on the church, *Lumen Gentium* (LG), declared: "From the wedlock of Christians there comes the family, in which new citizens of human society are born. ... The family is, so to speak, the domestic Church" (n.11).

[2] LG n.35.

[3] Frits Staal, *Discovering the Vedas: Origins, Mantras, Rituals, Insights* (New Delhi: Penguin Books, 2008), 53. According to the Hindu belief, the sage, Yajnavalkya received the Vedic mantras directly from the sun, indicating the timelessness of the Vedas.

[4] Frits Staal, 305-306.

[5] Aloysius Pieris, *Love Meets Wisdom: A Christian Experience of Buddhism* (Maryknoll, NY: Orbis Books, 1988), 67.

[6] Alois Pieris, *Love Meets Wisdom*, 104.

[7] Confucius, Doctrine of the Mean, 15:2.3. Cf *On Being Human in the Changing Realities of Asia,* FABC Office of Theological Concerns, FABC Papers, 133, March 2011, 6.

[8] Mircea Eleade, *Patterns in Comparative Religion* (London: Sheed and Ward, 1958), 253-56.

[9] John Paull II, *Ecclesia in America,* 1999, no.55.

[10] Federation of Asian Bishops' Conferences (FABC), *The Asian Family Towards a Culture of Integral Life,* (Statement of the 8th FABC Plenary Assembly, Daejeon, Korea: August 17-23, 2004, no 6, in *FABC Papers No 111,* Hong Kong September 2004,7.

[11] Mircea Eleade, *From Primitives to Zen* (London: Collins, 1967), 165.

[12] The close knit nature of Asian family can be gauged from a text in *Bhagavad Gita.* Even at the moment of losing everything including his kingdom due to deception, Arjuna asks Lord Krishna who prompts him to go to war against his uncle and cousins: "Therefore, O Madhava! It is not befitting that we kill our relations, the sons of Dhrtarastra. How could one be happy by the slaughter of one's own kinsmen?" (BG 1.37)

[13] "FABC Plenary Assembly Final Document: The Asian Family Towards a Culture of Integral Life," no. 2. FABC Papers, No 111, 2004, 5).

[14] Ibid, n.1, p.5.

[15] It is a matter of interest to realize how Asian religions like Hinduism and Buddhism imparts religious knowledge to children, not primarily through religious schools but through the daily, weekly as well as yearly family religious celebrations.

[16] See Kuncheria Pathil, "New Ways of Being Church in Asia," in *Evangelizing in the Third Millennium,* Gregory Karotemprel et al. (eds) (Rajkot: Deepthi Publications, 2006), 83.

[17] Frits Staal, 53.

[18] Frits Staal, 54.

[19] FABC Papers No 111, p.16.

[20] Indian Theological Association, "Marriage and Family Today – An Indian Theological Search," (38th Annual Meeting 30 April – 3 May 2015 (Vazhoor, Kerala. Statement 2015), n. 1.

[21] FABC Paper No 111, p.13.

[22] FABC Declaration n.23, FABC Paper 111, 14.

[23] FABC Office of Theological Commission, *On Being Human in the Changing Realities of Asia,* FABC Paper No 133, 35.

[24] St Paul refers to these house churches in his letters (Rom 16:5, 10; 1Cor 16:15, 19; etc.)

[25] See Varkey Vithayathil, "Mission and Life of St. Thomas in India," in *The Thomapedia,* George Menchery (ed), Trivandrum: Thomapedia, 2000), 3.

[26] Ibid, 4.

[27] Cardinal Eugene Tisserant, *Eastern Christianity in India* (Calcutta: Orient Longmans, 1957), 6-7.

[28] See Indian Theological Association Statement 2015, n.47.

[29] Pope Francis, "Concluding Address to the Synod," in *Catholic Herald,* Saturday 24 October 2015.

Chapter - 9

Mission the Comprehensive Vision of Biblical and Theological Formation

This concluding chapter proposes that there is a compelling justification for an intra-communication within Christian sciences such as theology, biblical studies and other disciplines, centred on the divine mission to the world. The chapter examines the need for theological ideas and scriptural insights to dialogue among them so as to make the church ever fitted to be a worthy sacrament of God's reaching out to the world.

It is only stating the obvious that the church at its earliest stage was missionary by its very call, as it experienced itself as the continuation of Jesus' mission (Jn 20:21). Mission was an overflow of its Christ experience (1Jn 1:1–4). The Acts of the Apostles tells us how the believers, filled with the holy spirit, spoke the word of God, with boldness (4:31). When the community was scattered following the martyrdom of Stephen, they went about preaching the word (8:4), some of whom, men of Cyprus and Cyrene, 'coming to Antioch spoke to the Gentiles (Greeks) also, preaching the Lord Jesus' (11.20). This way the ordinary Christians gave rise to the first Gentile community, and not St Paul as it is often thought to be. Similarly, Origen (c.185–254) writing in the third century, disproving the accusations of the enemy of the church, Celsus, agrees with him on the point that the Christian faith, in fact, was spread by the illiterate, women, workers of leather and wool and such common people, which again, confirms how every Christian was involved in mission.[1] As a matter of fact, except for St Paul, and a few others, we do not come across full time evangelizers in the early church. This chapter argues that theological education today has to help the Christian to retrieve this basic Christian call for our times and, hence, mission has to be the integrating principle of the various theological disciplines. Theological disciplines cannot remain mere academic shareholders, contributing to the academic industry.

Biblical Studies

Christopher J. H. Wright starts his massive volume on mission, stating: 'Mission is what the Bible is all about.'[2] The Bible presents the worldview for the Christian life and engagement in the world, sustaining an integral sense of existence in the world, generating and supporting Christian identity and orientation. It is foundational for any Christian activity and life.

The Bible tells how the God of the Bible, by nature, is a God of ecstasy, standing out of God's self, reaching out in creation and calling humans to covenantal relationships. The Bible shows us, through the many instances of Moses, Aaron, Joshua, Judges, the Prophets, and many others, as well as the call of Israel as a nation, that the divine call is not so much a privilege as a call to service. Thus the whole Bible is a dialogue of love, even as history is a history of divine self-reaching out in love. It is not a truth-affair as it was interpreted to be, that is to say it contains all the truths that humans are to believe, or a basis for all the fine-tuned dogmas and doctrines.

This is clearly spelt out in the Christ-event. The incarnate word is the manifestation of divine love in a personal form, so that all those who come into contact with him can have an experience of God (Jn 12: 45; 14:9; Lk 7:22). He becomes a prism that resolves divine love in concrete human experiences. He is Emmanuel, God with us (Mt 1:23). John describes this through verbs from two semantic fields: the terminology of movement and the terminology of task. While verbs such as 'sent', 'come', 'go', 'return', 'descend', 'ascend', 'leave', etc., belong to the first, others such as, 'to do the work', 'to bear fruit', 'to listen', 'to do the will', 'to harvest', 'to judge', and others, are of the second category. Jesus is not on a rescue operation, but is sent by God to make God's presence real, to bring in God's reign. All this is captured by Peter through his summarizing phrase, 'he went about doing good' (Act 10:38). Hence, the ministry of Jesus is the focal point through which Jesus manifested God's other-centeredness. His suffering, death and resurrection are to be seen in the light of his ministry, as Peter reminds us (Acts 2:36), rather than using the ministry to prove the historicity of the resurrection.

The resurrection is the capstone event in Jesus' ministry and the formative experience of the disciples. The experience of the resurrected Lord convinced the early church of the identity of Jesus as the Messiah and hence the son of God, in the light of which they begin to proclaim him and his ministry. Here we become aware of the reality of the universal mission, in contrast to mission in the Old Testament and even the mission of the earthly Jesus. Though there are universalistic trends in the Old Testament, there was no missionary activity in Judaism except some isolated reaching out to the non-Jews. Similarly, for all his openness to the Gentiles, Jesus too confined himself to fellow Jews. What brought about the radical change was the disciples' experience of the risen Lord. Biblical studies have to exploit the implications of this even for today.

The New Testament emerged from a community that was a missionary movement, and most of it was written by people engaged in mission, and what was written was to serve the cause of mission. As Martin Kahler reminds us, 'The New Testament writers were not scholars who had the leisure to research the evidence before they put pen to paper. Rather, they wrote in the context of an 'emergency situation', of a church which, because of its missionary encounter with the world, was forced to theologize.'[3]

In the New Testament, Jesus is not another God to be adored, displacing all others, but is the presence of God, Emmanuel (Mt 1:23). This is actualized through his words and deeds, making it possible for him to invite others 'to come and see' (Jn 1:39) and to follow him (Jn 21:19; Mk 1:17, 20 and parallels). The New Testament shows it is following Jesus in his ministry that makes one a Christian rather than any belief system or cult. This is formally expressed in Mk 3:14–15. Exegetical studies must be guided by a 'mission-generating'[4] hermeneutic. Interestingly, Jesus, despite all our claims about him and our preoccupation with all sorts of Christological theses, hardly ever talks about himself or proclaims himself, especially in the synoptic gospels. Even in the fourth gospel Jesus is God-centred and his food is to do the will of the father and to accomplish his work (Jn 4:34). The 'Our Father', the only prayer Jesus taught his disciples, is neither addressed to Jesus nor does it mention his name. His message is the arrival of God's reign and he is busy in manifesting it. As Marcus Borg underlines, Jesus' message is not about believing a set of doctrines about him, rather it is about the coming of God's reign, conveyed through words and deeds.[5] This, in turn, must prompt our study of the gospels to follow him in his mission.

Biblical studies has to empower one to mediate the vision of Jesus for our times and context. We need a 'postal code' interpretation of the Bible; that is, interpretation according to the specific concrete situation. Lucien Legrand in his book on Mission in the Bible narrates how his personal journey of unravelling the Bible was a pilgrimage of mission along with humanity with all its hopes and agonies.[6]

Luke's introductions to both the gospel as well as to the Acts of the Apostles are very significant. Luke wants to record the faith experience of the primitive community into a written form, despite the fact that writing was a tedious and expensive affair then (Lk 1:1–4; Act 1:1–2). Jesus himself had not left any written matter and the Jesus movement was essentially oral. In his introduction Luke says how he wants to render a written account in good Greek of what the preachers were speaking in Aramaic or Hebrew, 'to leave an orderly and reliable record of the events that had happened fifty years earlier at the beginning of the Jesus movement'.[7] Gispert-Sauch draws our attention further to how Luke's work would 'guide the living memory of the community and help it grow through history'.[8] It could be said that Luke wanted the readers to have a direct experience of the faith. In other words, through the two volume work, Luke wanted to articulate the basis of the Jesus movement. The written text serves as the vehicle to return to Jesus as the initiator of the movement, and its earliest history, so that the readers at any time can retrieve the same for their times and places, without the danger of the oral tradition getting lost in distant memory.

Biblical studies may not forget this purpose and the mandate to carry on the initial breakthrough to contemporary times and narrate the wonderful works of God to confront the women and men of our times. Scripture, thus, was an instrument to reflect on the life of Jesus Christ and God's activity in him, so that Christians could experience Christ and God, an experience frequently described as mystagogy. This was sidetracked with the onslaught of Aristotelian philosophy, with its emphasis on intellectual clarity. Though the reformers rightly emphasized the role of the Bible in Christian life, they used it primarily for evangelizing the papists! The counter-reformation used the bible mainly for defending dogmas in the form of scholastic theses.

Even today many scripture scholars tend to indulge in text analysis without much concern for the ground reality, and the original missionary purpose, making a lot of biblical output a part of the academic industry with little bearing on the mission of the church. Frequently we come across the situation of biblical scholarship becoming highly specialized and sophisticated, with little time and interest for the basic function of the Bible, sharing the good news.

Though exegesis has its own rights as an independent science, and thus an exegete's purpose need not be identical with that of the missionary, it should serve Christian living, which is ultimately missionary. An exegete's aim is faithful repetition in our language of what the biblical author is saying, but in doing so the exegete cannot prescind from the author's religious purposes. It is here that the link between exegetical study and mission is manifested. The Bible is normative for mission in so far as it is the narrative of the divine self-reaching out and the divine call to humans to be sharers in this mission.

Exegesis can be descriptive and secular and yet its theological interpretation has one purpose: to germinate or foster faith, to make faith meaningful to contemporary persons. As Elisabeth Schussler Fiorenza has argued, biblical scholars must move beyond the preoccupation with the text's original context to bring the insights of the Bible to bear upon the contemporary situation in the world.[9]

Biblical studies have an important role to play even with regard to the various expressions of mission today. Interfaith dialogue can go a long way by means of the insight that we all worship the same God despite different descriptions of God. Since the days of St. Anselm of Canterbury the satisfaction theory of the atonement was seen as the reason for the incarnation of Jesus who won human salvation by his death on the cross, limiting salvation only to the followers of Jesus Christ. Yet Jesus himself refers to his death as a political process of killing (Mk 10:33–34). Crucifixion was a terrorizing execution, used as a deterrent. The death predictions of Jesus are associated with his being raised to life. Death is not the end but being raised from the dead, which could be described as God's affirmation of Jesus as his Messiah; an affirmation that God did make at the time of Jesus' baptism as well as his transfiguration. The God whom Jesus Christ addressed as abba, and whose reign was his primary concern, was the God of Abraham, Isaac and Jacob (Mt 22:32 and parallel). He is the God of all and all those who do the will of God are Jesus' brothers and sisters (Mk. 3:34–35). Scripture can help us to free ourselves from dogmatic presumptions about God, making God a Christian monopoly.

This has significance for the Christian perception of other religious traditions and our mission in the context of religious pluralism. The whole theology of the vicarious suffering of Jesus, and the salvation presumed to have been accomplished by that, and the consequent emphasis on mission ad gentes need to be re-examined. Jesus refers the man asking him how to attain eternal life to the Decalogue and not to his death on the cross (Mk 10:17–20 and parallel). As Heikki Raisanen has pointed out, Jesus seeks 'sinners', but does not deny the existence of those who are 'not in need of a physician' (Mk 2:17). 'Sins are spoken of in the plural; they are individual acts which can be forgiven (Lk 11:4 etc.).'[10] Without going into detail, I would plead that biblical studies has the unfailing task of taking into account the original diversity of Christian convictions and their implications for mission today. What does it mean for the Christian being sent into the world today? Is it geared only or even primarily to a conversion-oriented mission? This has been a topic of discussion in the preceding chapters.

In the same way the church's service to human rights, and justice and peace today can be helped by the study of the biblical prophets and by the examination of the ministry of Jesus. Despite the few dissenting texts in the New Testament where Jesus' death is interpreted in vicarious terms, the gospels present his death as a typical fate of a prophet and not as a death invested with soteriological meanings.

Theological Studies and Mission

What we have been saying about biblical studies is equally true of theological studies as well. The primary purpose of theological formation is to enable, to equip the participants intellectually, emotionally, socially and spiritually to participate in God's reaching out to the world, God's mission to the world. Theology is not just an informative discipline, it is also a performative discipline, seeking commitment. It is an informed reflection on the Word of God in context, leading to commitment. If theology does not lead one to mission, there will be a lot of 'unlearning' in the field of mission. Shedding the learnt material as useless would be unjustifiable, if not also failing in accountability, in so far as it is a waste of precious resources.

Theology becomes an exploration into the meaning of discipleship today. Thus, it is an ideology for mission; the rationality and justification for mission. Theology is operational and participative, participating in God's dealings with the world, to transform it from the non-kingdom situation to the kingdom situation. Theology must open one to synchronize oneself with God's agenda for the world. The missionary content and orientation gives theology its Christian identity. Theology, I would suggest, unpacks the Christian call to follow Jesus today, thus making it experiential and transformative. Theology spells out how mission merges revelation with the context.

As the Theological Education and Formation Group of the Edinburgh 2010 Mission Conference pointed out, western theological formation was shaped when Christendom in Europe did not feel the need for Christian mission because it knew only itself.[11] The Council of Trent introduced a systematic theological programme as part of the priestly formation in the Catholic tradition. However, it was heavily doctrinal and indoctrinating, based on the Summa Theologica of Thomas Aquinas. The Protestants continued the trend, but patterned by Friedrich Schleiermacher's (1768–1834) fourfold scheme: scripture, church history, systematic theology and practical theology. Eventually reflection on mission was appended to practical theology.

The Bible shows how the Babylonian exile brought about a fresh understanding of God for the Israelites and how the spread of the gospel to the Greek context prepared the way for a new understanding of Jesus as the Lord, from that of the Christ. To the Athenians St Paul presented Jesus as 'a man through whom God established justice', without any reference to his being the Messiah, for the core issue for them was justice (Act 17:31). This is a challenge for theology to prepare a deeper foundation for the understanding of the gospel for the world of our times. Theology has to make Christians aware of their duty not just of fulfilling the city council's demand for creating a multicultural society, but to go beyond to make it truly a divine household, where all are equally accepted and respected.

It can also happen that our theology is framed in an outdated understanding of revelation so that it is unable to facilitate Christians to enter into a meaningful dialogue and collaboration with the followers of other religious traditions. If theology fails to enable Christians to follow Jesus Christ in the pluralistic context meaningfully, they may abandon faith or may tend to describe themselves as 'nobodies'. Australian society, for instance, attaches high value on innovation and relevance. Frequently our theology fails to meet with this expectation, leading to unchangeable liturgy and practices that the majority find irrelevant.

Theology can show how pluralism is within the divine design and hence not a threat to Christian faith, which in itself is a call to dedicate oneself for the sake of others. This, in turn, encourages a mission of interfaith dialogue and collaboration for the realization of the divine reign.

Theology reminds us how we are 'on the way', helping us to create a safe-zone to grow in our relation with God and the neighbour. Authentic discipleship is ecstatic, reaching outward. To sustain that spirit of discipleship we need the constant tethering of scripture and theology. Christian community is not one that constantly demands that others come to it, but it also goes out, in the spirit of Jesus Christ or that of the prophet (Isaiah 65:17–21), so that there is no more the sound of weeping or the sound of crying, but of joy and gladness. If our theological and scriptural study does not prompt us to be involved in wiping out suffering and to put a smile on the face of the suffering, it is sterile and similar to salt that has lost its saltiness.

The church is an event, a movement of reaching out, continuing the divine self- reaching out. It is not primarily an institution, fortified with creeds and dogmas. True, today this institutional dimension cannot be ignored, as any other human movement. However, as an event, the primary concern of the church is the reaching out of itself to those who are outside the walls; taking the church where the people are. This reaching out has to be incarnational, as the word became flesh in a specific cultural context, to be made present for all cultural contexts through the activity of the community of the disciples. Theological formation shapes our mission. Missional imagination animates theology, providing unity of purpose and commitment.

Theology has to be focused on God and God's activities in the world. The world and its problems and opportunities are vital to theological studies. This renders contextuality to theology, making it relevant and meaningful. The late Pope John XXIII, invited theologians to be experts in reading the signs of the times. It is the DNA (Discipleship Narrative Account) of theology.

Theology becomes the inspiration for the transformation of the world in anticipation of the divine reign.

Theological education has to be crafted carefully so as to respond to the need of witnessing to the Lord Jesus, in the given context, in contrast to the earlier, more or less uniform pattern, that had the primary purpose of creating institutional administrators described as pastoral leaders. It had a more or less stable understanding. The professors could predetermine the need of their students to function within the institutional churches. This is no longer the case, with the changed situation where mission takes priority; the outside world is more significant and this world cannot be foreseen. Rather than providing answers, theological education makes one responsible, that is, capable of responding to the context relevantly and meaningfully. Theology must underline how Christian baptism is a 'general ordination to Christian service'.[12]

Our theological formation is not just a preparation for a future mission, somewhere out there, or in a parish to which we may be assigned; rather, it should fit us for an engagement already now. It should help us to understand how we are sent to each other and to our context already now. We are not encased in the theological college, cut off from the world, but we stand constantly in rapport with our context. This, in turn, can influence our behaviour and lifestyle, colouring our judgements, perceptions, decisions, both individually and collectively. Already now we can become catalysts for change.

A related point is the dichotomy between the sacred and the secular. For us there is sacredness to the secular even as the sacred can spill into the secular. This is linked with the whole dynamic of the calling–sending–transforming witnessing of Christian discipleship. It is an integral whole. It is a call to become a comforting presence to the suffering, an affirming presence to the unloved and lonely, a supporting presence to the marginalized. Thus our theological formation becomes a fulcrum for us to be, in the words of Walter Kasper, a 'dialogical sacrament' to the world.

We need not compartmentalize theological disciplines for the sake of mission; rather, mission can become the animating principle of every theological discipline. Each discipline must become centrifugal. Service to the world must be the animating principle. If not, theology will lead to careerism, seeking to excel in the field as a means of earning a name for oneself, imitating industry.

A doctrine-oriented theology makes the Roman Curia distrustful of the Asian and Latin American theologians rather than appreciating the struggles of these theologians to respond to their contexts by manifesting the loving God who made God-self present in the ministry of Jesus Christ in the particular context of the Jewish expectations, with the mandate to make it present to every culture.

Theology has to take into consideration not only the community of the believers, but also general society and its culture. This vision of ad extra makes theology essentially missionary. It is concerned about the betterment of the quality of life for all. It is not only a question of their material well-being but also answering the questions of those dissatisfied with religion. Theology becomes the inter- section of divine revelation and human society.

In the context of religious pluralism as well as the talk of 'multiple belonging', theology has to spell out how the God Christians call upon, and whom Jesus Christ made present in his ministry, is the one who is the universal origin and goal of the whole of humankind, who nevertheless, chose a people to be his instrument, to serve as the light to the world. This election is to be balanced by the hope that all the elect will be illumined by the glory of God. Christian theology of other religions is only what Christians think about them, and not what others are attaining or attempting to attain. Jacques Matthey in his article, 'Towards a Missiology Inspired by the Book of Proverbs', celebrates Wisdom that invites all humans to understand and follow the path of life, and suggests, 'Mission must first encourage a following of the inspiration given universally to each one by God the creator.'[13]

Christianity as a religion of remembering and sharing God's saving love in Jesus Christ is very much helped by scripture and theology. They have played a leading role all through the history of the church's collaboration in God's work. Until the rise of specific missiological chairs and faculties, towards the beginning of the 20th century, the missionary role of theological education was not generally perceived, though on the positive side, involvement in mission was more the result of the inspiration of the spirit. David Bosch describes the situation:

If mission was studied at all, it was usually as part of practical theology, as it was largely a matter of technique or practical application; or it was offered as a totally separate subject, as if it had little to do with the other 'streams,' or it was an optional subject, competing with preaching, pastoral counselling or liturgics, for the learners' attention.[14]

With Vatican II for the Catholics, and with the many Mission Conferences of the World Council of Churches (WCC), theological education geared towards mission has become common. The identity of the church and its mission formed the core of Second Vatican Council. The Council declared how the church is missionary by its very nature (Ad Gentes 2) and every conciliar document deals with one or other aspect of mission. The Council's description of the church as the Sacrament of the kingdom (Lumen Gentium 1) and as the People of God (Lumen Gentium Chapter II) retrieved the significance of Baptism as the basic sacrament of mission, and not Ordination.[15]

The Edinburgh 2010 Study Paper on theological education expressed it succinctly:

The rediscovery of the missionary nature of the church in conciliar ecumenical movement in the '60s, the evangelical renewal of the Lausanne movement in the '70s, and the post Vatican II encyclicals on the missionary nature of the church, have had a profound impact on redefining the missionary task perspectives of theological education.[16]

Concluding Remarks

This chapter has shown how the divine mission to the world is the integrating principle of all biblical and theological studies. The Bible is the narration of God's reaching out to the world, and theological education must synchronize the Christian to God's agenda for the world. Theological disciplines are not academic shareholders contributing to the academic industry. Rather, they must empower one to mediate the vision of Jesus for our history. Mission is the sustaining cause of the church in so far as it is instituted to continue God's reaching out to the world in Jesus Christ. Mission determines its biblical and theological formation.

Endnotes

1 Origen, Contra Celsum, III, 49–55.

2 Christopher J. H. Wright, *Mission of God* (Nottingham: InterVarsity, 2008), 29.

3 Martin Kahler, *Schriften zur Christologie und Mission* (Munich: Kaiser Verlag, 1971/ 1908), 189.

4 Wright, *Mission of God*, 61.

5 Marcus J. Borg, *Meeting Jesus in Mark* (London: SPCK, 2011), 73–74.

6 Lucien Legrand, *Unity and Plurality: Mission in the Bible*, (Maryknoll: Orbis, 1990), ix–xv.

7 George Gispert-Sauch, 'Changing Languages and the Gospel Mission', Vidyajyoti 77 (2013), 97–100, see p. 98.

8 Gispert-Sauch, 'Changing Languages', 99.

9 Elizabeth Schussler Fiorenza, 'The ethics of interpretation: De-centering biblical scholarship', Journal of Biblical Literature 107 (1988), 3–12.

10 Heikki Raisanen, 'A Plea for Pluralism: Reflections on Mission Studies by a Biblical Scholar', Swedish Missiological Themes 99 (2011), 395–417, see p. 399

11 Daryl Balia and Kirsteen Kim (eds), Edinburgh 2010, Vol II: *Witnessing to Christ Today* (Oxford: Regnum Books International, 2010), 153.

12 Darrell L. Guder, 'The Christians' Callings in the World', New Theology Review 24 (2011), 6–16, see p. 13.

13 Jacques Matthey, 'Towards a Missiology Inspired by the Book of Proverbs', in Emma Wild-Wood and Peniel Rajkumar (eds), *Foundations for Mission* (Regnum Edinburgh Series 13; Oxford: Wipf & Stock Publishers, 2013), 69–84, see p. 77.

14 David Bosch, 'Theological Education in Missionary Perspective', Missiology 11 (1982), 13–34, see p. 19.

15 Stephen B. Bevans and Roger P. Schroeder, *Constants in Context: A Theology of Mission for Today* (Maryknoll, NY: Orbis, 2004), 97.

16 'Documentation', International Review of Mission 99 (2010), 86–158, see p. 129.

www.ingramcontent.com/pod-product-compliance
Lightning Source LLC
LaVergne TN
LVHW091706190726
843493LV00001B/175